In Essence One, in Persons Three

To Stephen J. Wellum,
a dear friend and colleague,
and gifted Trinitarian theologian

STUDIES IN BAPTIST HISTORY

IN ESSENCE ONE, IN PERSONS THREE

The doctrine of the Trinity in Particular Baptist life and thought, 1640s–1840s

Edited by
MICHAEL A.G. HAYKIN
with ROY M. PAUL

In Essence One, in Persons Three

Copyright © 2022 Hesed and Emet Publishing

All rights reserved. This book may not be reproduced, in whole or in part, without written permission from the publishers.

Unless otherwise indicated, all Scripture quotations are from The ESV® Bible (The Holy Bible, English Standard Version®), copyright © 2001 by Crossway, a publishing ministry of Good News Publishers. Used by permission. All rights reserved.

H&E Academic, West Lorne, Ontario
www.hesedandemet.com

Paperback ISBN: 978-1-77484-090-0
Ebook ISBN: 978-1-77484-091-7

Contents

Introduction 1
   Michael A.G. Haykin

1. "Three subsistences ... one substance":
The Doctrine of the Trinity in the *Second London Confession*.......... 7
   Steve Weaver

2. Scripture Demonstrations of the Holy Trinunity:
Benjamin Keach's Defense of the Doctrine of the Trinity............. 27
   Jonathan W. Arnold

3. The Salters' Hall Controversy:
Heresy, Subscription, or Both?.. 45
   Jesse F. Owens

4. John Gill (1697–1771) and the Eternal Begotten Word of God .. 69
   Jonathan E. Swan

5. "Co-equal, co-essential, and co-eternal":
Anne Dutton on the Trinity 99
   Michael A.G. Haykin

6. "Not the same God":
Alexander Carson and the Ulster Trinitarian Controversy......... 115
   Ian Hugh Clary

Contributors.. 143
Scripture Index 145
Index... 146

Introduction

Michael A.G. Haykin

Until the seventeenth and eighteenth centuries, the Trinitarian orthodoxy of the Ancient Church, which was encapsulated in the Niceno-Constantinopolitan creed (381), remained basically unchallenged. Even during the theological tumult of the Reformation, this vital area of Christian belief did not come into widespread dispute, though there were a few, like Miguel Servet (1511–1553) and the Italians, Lelio Francesco Sozzini (1525–1562) and his nephew Fausto Sozzini (1539–1604), who rejected Trinitarianism for a Unitarian perspective on the Godhead. However, as Sarah Mortimer has argued in her ground-breaking study of seventeenth-century English Socinianism, in the century after the Reformation the Socinian understanding of human beings as "inquiring, reasoning and active individuals who must take responsibility for their own spiritual lives" did come to play a critical role in undermining the way that "Trinitarian communities" in England had established theological boundaries for themselves.[1] This was part of a growing tide of rationalism in the seventeenth century and the one following that led to what P. Dixon has called a "fading of the trinitarian imagination" and to the doctrine coming under heavy attack.[2] Informed by the Enlightenment's confidence

---

[1] Sarah Mortimer, *Reason and Religion in the English Revolution. The Challenge of Socinianism* (Cambridge: Cambridge University Press, 2010), 240–241.

[2] Paul Dixon, *"Nice and Hot Disputes": The Doctrine of the Trinity in the Seventeenth Century* (London/New York, NY: T & T Clark, 2003), 212. See also William C. Placher, *The Domestication of Transcendence. How Modern Thinking about God Went Wrong* (Louisville, KY: Westminster John Knox Press, 1996), 164–178.

in the omnicompetence of human reason, increasingly the intellectual *mentalité* of this era either dismissed the doctrine of the Trinity as a philosophical and unbiblical construct of the post-Apostolic Church, and turned to classical Arianism as an alternate perspective or simply ridiculed it as utterly illogical and argued for Deism or Socinianism.[3]

Now, what is amazing is that this critical battle over Trinitarianism in the seventeenth and eighteenth centuries—its outcome would help determine the shape of later thinking about Christianity's God—is passed over in utter silence by the vast majority of modern studies of the history of this doctrine. Typically, these studies leap over the seventeenth and eighteenth centuries, moving directly from the Trinitarian reflections of a Reformer like John Calvin (1509–1564) to various nineteenth or twentieth-century theologians.[4] The impression is thus given that between the Reformation and liberal theologians like Friedrich Schleiermacher (1768–1834) there had been little of significance written on Trinitarian doctrine. To anyone familiar, though, with the writings of the English Puritan John Owen (1616–1683) or the New England theologian of revival Jonathan Edwards (1703–1758) on the Trinity, for example, this is a highly questionable claim. In fact, as the following essays demonstrate, the doctrine of the Trinity was *the* central issue at stake in the encounter between the Enlightenment, beginning in the latter half of the seventeenth century, and Christian orthodoxy.

These essays are focused on one Dissenting community, namely, the Particular Baptists, who are often regarded as being marginal to the history of Anglophone Christianity in the long eighteenth century. And yet, throughout this era, the Particular

---

[3] G. L. Bray, "Trinity" in *New Dictionary of Theology*, ed. Sinclair B. Ferguson, David F. Wright, and J.I. Packer (Downers Grove, IL; Leicester: InterVarsity Press, 1988), 694.

[4] Dixon, *Nice and Hot Disputes*, xi–xii, n.1.

Michael A.G. Haykin

Baptists in the British Isles tenaciously confessed a Trinitarian understanding of the Godhead and so, while other communities, such as the English Presbyterians and the General Baptists largely ceased to be Trinitarian, the Particular Baptists continued to regard themselves, and that rightly, as a Trinitarian community. In the words of the London Baptist minister Benjamin Wallin (1711-1782), the doctrine of the Trinity is, the "first and grand principle of revealed truth and the gospel."[5] In 1690, the London Baptist layman Isaac Marlow (1649-1719), for example, had published a treatise on the Trinity in which he stated his conviction that of those elements of divine truth that redound most to the glory of God and best further the fellowship of believers, "the blessed doctrine of the holy Trin-unity is the chiefest."[6] Nearly fifty years later, the renowned preacher Joseph Stennett II (1692-1758), who was a pillar of this community, similarly affirmed that "the doctrine of the ever blessed Trinity, is of the greatest importance to his [that is, God's] glory."[7] And when the members of Chertsey Street Baptist Church in Guildford, Surrey, renewed their church covenant in 1744, they asserted their corporate belief in "the doctrine of the Blessed Trinity; viz. That the Godhead consist in Father, Son and Holy Ghost, and that these three are one living and true God; the same in substance, equal in power and glory."[8]

Unlike the Anglican Church, in which there was a prayer-book and a liturgy, both of which were suffused with Trinitarianism,[9]

---

[5] Benjamin Wallin, *The eternal Existence of the Lord Jesus Christ considered and improved* (London, 1766), iv-v.

[6] Isaac Marlow, *A Treatise of the Holy Trinunity* [sic] (London, 1690), [i-ii].

[7] Joseph Stennett, *The Christian Strife for the Faith of the Gospel* (London, 1738), 78, cited Roger Hayden, "The Contribution of Bernard Foskett" in William H. Brackney and Paul S. Fiddes with John H. Y. Briggs, ed., *Pilgrim Pathways: Essays in Baptist History in Honour of B.R. White* (Macon GA: Mercer University Press, 1999), 197.

[8] "Grace Church Guildford History" (https://www.gracechurchguildford.org.uk/wp-content/uploads/2020/10/Grace-Church-Guildford-History.pdf; accessed July 7, 2021).

[9] Dixon, *Nice and Hot Disputes*, 215-216.

the Particular Baptists had no such resources to use to buttress the Trinitarian faith of their churches. Yet, there were theologians like the London pastor John Gill (1697-1771), of whom Olin C. Robison has rightly stated: "he was the living symbol of Particular Baptist thought during the middle fifty years of the eighteenth century."[10] Gill is often critiqued as a High-Calvinist whose opposition to the free offer of the Gospel helped to undermine Particular Baptist growth for much of his lifetime. The details of Gill's High-Calvinism are a controverted issue that is not easily resolved. But what is certain is the influence of his unflagging commitment to the doctrine of the Trinity. Gill's *The Doctrine of the Trinity Stated and Vindicated* was an effective defence of the fact that there is

> but one God; that there is a plurality in the Godhead; that there are three divine Persons in it; that the Father is God, the Son God, and the Holy Spirit God; that these are distinct in Personality, the same in substance, equal in power and glory.[11]

The heart of this treatise was incorporated into Gill's *Body of Doctrinal Divinity* (1769) which became for many Particular Baptist pastors their major theological resource, and thus Gill played a central role in keeping a Trinitarian faith front and centre in the minds of many Baptist leaders. As John Rippon (1751-1836), Gill's successor at his London church, bore testimony to Gill's faithfulness to Trinitarian orthodoxy:

> The Doctor not only watched over his *people*, "with great affection, fidelity, and love;" but he also watched his *pulpit* also. He would not, if he knew it, admit any one to preach

---

[10] Olin C. Robison, "The Legacy of John Gill," *The Baptist Quarterly* 24, no.3 (1971-1972): 122.

[11] John Gill, *The Doctrine of the Trinity Stated and Vindicated*, 2nd ed. (London, 1752), 166-167.

for him, who was either cold-hearted to the doctrine of the Trinity; or who *denied* the divine filiation of the Son of God; or who *objected* to conclude his prayers with the usual *doxology* to Father, Son, and Holy Spirit, as three equal Persons in the one Jehovah. Sabellians, Arians, and Socinians, he considered as real enemies of the cross of Christ. They *dared* not ask him to preach, nor *could* he in conscience, permit them to officiate for him. He conceived that, by this uniformity of conduct, he adorned the pastoral office.[12]

He did more than "adorn the pastoral office." Through the written word he helped shepherd the English Particular Baptist community along the pathway of orthodoxy. Due to his commitment to Trinitarian orthodoxy, when the fire of revival began to burn among the Particular Baptists in the closing decades of the eighteenth century, there were coals of orthodoxy to kindle and be enflamed.

The essays in this book not only deal with Gill's Trinitarianism, but also document the Trinitarian Faith of the Particular Baptist from their origins and earliest confessions in the mid-seventeenth century to the mid-nineteenth century when the Irish Particular Baptist Alexander Carson (1776–1844) defended the doctrine against Arian Presbyterians. Apart from Prof. Clary's article on Carson and my essay on Anne Dutton (1692–1765), the other essays all had their origins in papers given at a conference sponsored by the Andrew Fuller Center for Baptist Studies on the campus of the Southern Baptist Theological Seminary in Louisville, Kentucky, in 2019, the three-hundredth anniversary of the Salters' Hall Synod, a key turning-point in the Trinitarian debates of the eighteenth century. All of the essays, apart from my essay on Dutton, have also appeared in an issue of *Perichoresis: The*

---

[12] John Rippon, *A Brief Memoir of the Life and Writings of the Late Rev. John Gill, D.D.* (1838, Harrisonburg, VA: Gano Books, 1992), 127–128.

In Essence One, in Persons Three

Theological Journal of Emanuel University, and appear here by kind permission.

1
"Three subsistences ... one substance": The Doctrine of the Trinity in the *Second London Confession*[1]

Steve Weaver

Both the General and Particular branches of the seventeenth-century Baptists faced challenges in key areas of historic Christianity. Each group had prominent leaders in their movements embrace substandard positions on both the Trinity and Christology. For the General Baptists, Matthew Caffyn (1628–1714)[2] would lead many astray with his heretical teachings concerning the nature of the humanity of Jesus. Caffyn denied that Jesus had received his human flesh from the Virgin Mary. Among the Particular Baptists, Thomas Collier (*fl.* 1634–1691)[3] proved to be a moving target in regard to his orthodoxy. Collier denied the historic understanding of the Trinity during the 1640s, passing through a period of orthodoxy in the 1650s and 1660s, before finally rejecting original sin, limited atonement and the incarnation in the 1670s. Both

---

[1] This essay is a lightly edited and condensed extract from my previously published work on Hercules Collins, G. Stephen Weaver, Jr., *Orthodox, Puritan, Baptist: Hercules Collins (1647–1702) and Particular Baptist Identity in Early Modern England* (Göttingen: Vandenhoek & Ruprecht, 2015). Used with permission from the publisher. A version of this essay was also published in the *Puritan Reformed Journal* 9, no. 2 (July 2017): 211–225.

[2] For a brief biographical sketch, see Jim Spivey, "Caffyn, Matthew," in *DNB*, ed. H.C.G. Matthew and Brian Harrison (Oxford: Oxford University Press, 2004).

[3] For a brief biographical sketch, see Stephen Wright, "Collier, Thomas," in *DNB*, ed. H.C.G. Matthew and Brian Harrison (Oxford: Oxford University Press, 2004). Collier's name is sometimes spelled "Collyer" in his published works. Throughout this essay I have used the spelling "Collier."

Caffyn and Collier would receive responses from capable pastor-theologians within their own respective traditions. While Matthew Caffyn received a thorough response from Thomas Monck, this essay will explore the Particular Baptist response to Thomas Collier. The essay will argue that Hercules Collins' often overlooked writings identify that he was consciously committed to the orthodox Trinitarianism and Christology of the Niceano-Constantinopolitan and Chalcedonian Creeds.

Collier and the Particular Baptist Response

Thomas Collier was a native of Somerset and a key leader in the Western Association's adoption of the Somerset Confession in 1656.[4] His career, however, was riddled with doctrinal instability.[5] In his Oxford dissertation on Collier, Richard Dale Land states "that there were only relatively brief periods of Collier's career when he was unquestionably orthodox by what the Particular Baptists themselves published as their theological standards, namely *Confession* (1644) and *Confession* (1677)."[6] Indeed, Michael A.G. Haykin has labeled the doctrinal defection of Collier as perhaps the most pressing reason for a new confession of faith in 1677.[7] In

---

[4] *A Confession Of The Faith of several Churches of Christ, In the Country of Somerset, and of some Churches in the Counties neer adjacent* (London: Henry Hills, 1656).

[5] For more on the career of Thomas Collier, see Richard Dale Land, "Doctrinal Controversies of English Particular Baptists (1644-1691) as Illustrated by the Career and Writings of Thomas Collier" (D.Phil. thesis, Regent's Park College, Oxford University, 1979). For detailed documentation of Collier's departure from Calvinist orthodoxy, see James M. Renihan, "Thomas Collier's Descent into Error: Collier, Calvinism, and the Second London Confession," *Reformed Baptist Theological Review* 1, no. 1 (January 2004): 67-83.

[6] Land, "Doctrinal Controversies of English Particular Baptists," 332.

[7] Michael A.G. Haykin, *Kiffen, Knollys, and Keach: Rediscovering our English Baptist Heritage* (Peterborough, ON, 2019), 112. Collier's defection was emblematic of a larger movement in seventeenth-century England, which included men such as John Biddle (1616-1662), that denied the deity of Christ and the Trinity. For a recent detailed study of this doctrinal controversy, see Paul C. H. Lim, *Mystery Unveiled: The Crisis of the Trinity in Early Modern England*, Oxford Studies in Historical Theology (Oxford: Oxford University Press, 2012). The 1690s saw the rise of English Deism through the writings of such men as Anthony Collins (1676-1729), Matthew Tindal

his 1674 *Body of Divinity*, Collier had denied the Calvinistic doctrine of particular redemption while asserting the eternality of the human nature of Christ.[8] In 1676, in a work titled *An Additional Word to the Body of Divinity*, Collier clarified his stance by strengthening his statements regarding the universal provision of the atonement, the eternality of the human nature of the Son and his refusal to use the term "person" as in the historic Christian orthodox formulation of the doctrine of the Trinity.[9] The latter rejection reflects Collier's teaching on the subject three decades prior. In 1648, for example, Collier had denied the historic orthodox understanding of the Trinity. Collier wrote that God

> is not, first, as some imagine, *Three Persons yet one God*, or three subsistings, distinguished though not divided; Its altogether impossible to distinguish God in this manner, and not divide him; thus to distinguish is to divide; for three persons are three not only distinguished, but divided: Some say there is, *God the Father, God the Son, and God the Holy Ghost, yet not three, but one God*; Let any one judge if here be not three Gods, if three then not one.[10]

In the words of Thomas Hall, an opponent of the Baptists, Collier was "a most dangerous and blasphemous Heretick," nothing less than an Arian, because he "denied the Trinity."[11] Although Hall

---

(1655-1733), and John Toland (1670-1722). For a brief synopsis of this development, see Gregg R. Allison, *Historical Theology: An Introduction to Christian Doctrine* (Grand Rapids: Zondervan, 2011), 113-114.

[8] Thomas Collier, *The Body of Divinity, Or, a Confession of Faith, Being the substance of Christianity: Containing the most Material things relating to Matters both of Faith and Practise* (London: Nath. Crouch, 1674), 117 and 31.

[9] Thomas Collier, *An Additional Word To The Body of Divinity, Or Confession Of Faith; Being the substance of Christianity* (London, 1676), 1-18.

[10] Thomas Collier, *A General Epistle, To The Universal Church of the First Born: Whose Names are written in Heaven* (London: Giles Calvert, 1648), 4.

[11] [Thomas Hall], *The Collier in his Colours: or, The Picture of a Collier* (London, 1652), in Hall's *The Font Guarded With XX Arguments* (London, 1652), 123, 125.

was aware that Collier's beliefs were not shared by the generality of the Calvinistic Baptists,[12] others were not so discerning and took Collier's views as representative of the whole of his one-time co-religionists. A response from the Particular Baptist community was therefore necessary. Nehemiah Coxe[13] offered one such response in his 1677 *Vindicae Veritas*.[14] Another response came the same year in the form of the *Second London Confession of Faith*,[15] which was likely composed by Coxe and his fellow Petty France co-pastor William Collins.[16] A largely overlooked response, however, came in the year 1680 from the pen of Hercules Collins.

Collins and An Orthodox Catechism

In 1680, Hercules Collins published his *An Orthodox Catechism*. This modified version of the historic Protestant Heidelberg Catechism was published, as stated on the title page: "For Preventing the Canker and Poison of Heresy and Error."[17] Collins was concerned with defending his fellow Baptists against charges of heresy while at the same time providing an instrument of instruction in order to prevent the spread of further false teaching among

---

[12] Hall, *The Collier in his Colours in The Font Guarded*, 121, 125.

[13] For a brief biographical sketch of Coxe, see James M. Renihan, "An Excellent and Judicious Divine: Nehemiah Coxe," *Reformed Baptist Theological Review* 4, no. 2 (July 2007): 61–78.

[14] Nehemiah Coxe, *Vinidicae Veritas, Or A Confutation Of The Heresies and Gross Errours Asserted by Thomas Collier In His Additional Word To His Body of Divinity* (London: Nath. Ponder, 1677).

[15] *A Confession Of Faith Put Forth by the Elders and Brethren Of many Congregations Of Christians (baptized upon Profession of their Faith) in London and the Country* (London: Benjamin Harris, 1677).

[16] An obscure reference is made in the minutes of the Petty France church on August 26, 1677, to the publication of a confession of faith. *Petty France Church Minute Book*, 6. This confession would be formally adopted by the General Assembly of Particular Baptists in 1689.

[17] H[ercules] Collins, *An Orthodox Catechism: Being the Sum of Christian Religion, Contained in the Law and Gospel* (London, 1680), title page. The text of this catechism, alongside the text of the Heidelberg Catechism, is also provided in James M. Renihan, *True Confessions: Baptist Documents in the Reformed Family* (Palmdale, CA: Reformed Baptist Academic Press, 2004).

their number. Thus, the catechism had both polemical and pastoral functions. As seen above, the polemical focus of the catechism was necessary due to the fact that one of the leading church planters of the Calvinistic Baptist community in the early decades of their movement, Thomas Collier, had brought the Baptists into disrepute. Collins wrote primarily, however, as a pastor to safeguard the congregation entrusted to him. The catechism was addressed very specifically to "the Church of Christ, who upon Confession of Faith have bin baptized, Meeting in *Old-Gravil-Lane London.*"[18] Having become the pastor of the Wapping congregation only four years earlier, Collins modified the Heidelberg so as to use as a tool in fulfilling his pastoral duties. A comparison of the two documents reveals a number of edits, a good number of which are best explained as Collins' attempts to make the catechism more accessible to his local congregation. Collins explicitly stated this concern for the spiritual nurture of the local congregation to which he ministered in the following benediction that concluded his "Preface" to the catechism: "And for those whom the Lord hath committed to my Charge, that the Eternal God may be your Refuge, and underneath you everlasting Arms; that Grace may be opened to your Hearts, and your hearts to Grace; that the blessing of the God of Abraham, Isaac and Jacob may be upon you, and the eternal Spirit may be with you, shall be the Prayer of your unworthy Brother, but more unworthy Pastor."[19] For Collins, orthodoxy was not just doctrine to be believed, it was truth to be defended and taught to those under his responsibility as pastor.

Use of the Creeds
The Heidelberg Catechism originally contained the Apostles' Creed. Collins, however, would follow the General Baptists' *An*

---

[18] Collins, *An Orthodox Catechism*, "The Preface;" Renihan, *True Confessions*, 236.
[19] Collins, *An Orthodox Catechism*, "The Preface;" Renihan, *True Confessions*, 238.

Orthodox Creed[20] in adding the Nicene and Athanasian Creeds.[21] Thus, what Harmon has said of the *Orthodox Creed* as a confession of faith can equally be said of the *Orthodox Catechism* as a catechism, namely that it is the "most explicit and thoroughgoing referencing of the patristic tradition" among Baptist catechisms.[22] In his preface to *An Orthodox Catechism*, Collins would explain his rationale for including the three creeds from the patristic tradition:

> *I have proposed* three Creeds *to your consideration, which ought thoroughly to be believed and embraced by all those that would be accounted Christians, viz. The* Nicene Creed, Athanasius his Creed, *and the* Creed *commonly called the* Apostles; *The last of which contains the sum of the Gospels; which is industriously opened and explained; and I beseech you do not slight it because of its Form, nor Antiquity, nor because supposed to be composed by Men; neither because some that hold it, maintain some Errors, or whose Conversation may not be correspondent to such fundamental Principles of Salvation; but take this for a perpetual Rule, That whatever is good in any, owned by any, whatever Error or Vice it may be mixed withal, the Good must not be rejected for the Error or Vice sake, but owned;*

---

[20] *An Orthodox Creed: Or, A Protestant Confession of Faith. Being An Essay to Unite, and Confirm all true Protestants in the Fundamental Articles of the Christian Religion, against the Errors and Heresies of the Church of Rome* (London, 1679). Complete text also found in William L. Lumpkin, *Baptist Confessions of Faith* (Valley Forge, PA: Judson Press, 1969), 297–334.

[21] Four pieces of evidence indicate that Collin was inspired by the *Orthodox Creed* in the formation of his *Orthodox Catechism*. First, most obviously, both documents contain the word "orthodox" in their titles. Second, Collins matches the three creeds of the *Orthodox Creed* by adding the Nicene and Athanasian Creeds to the already present Apostles Creed. Third, the wording of the final sentence of the Athanasian Creed in the *Orthodox Catechism* follows the unique wording found in the *Orthodox Creed* exactly: "This is the Catholick Faith, &c. Which, *every one should believe faithfully*." Cf. *Orthodox Creed*, 62; and *Orthodox Catechism*, 74; Renihan, *True Confessions*, 287. Fourth, Collins replicates word-for-word a marginal note on Christ's descent into hell in the Apostles Creed. Cf. *Orthodox Creed*, 57; and *Orthodox Catechism*, 16.

[22] Steven R. Harmon, *Towards Baptist Catholicity: Essays on Tradition and the Baptist Vision*, Studies in Baptist History and Thought 27 (Milton Keynes, England: Paternoster Press, 2006), 77.

commended, and accepted.[23]

Here we see that Collins assumed that the classic Trinitarian and Christological orthodoxy contained in the Apostles, Nicene and Athanasian Creeds would "*be believed and embraced by all those that would be accounted Christians.*" Their content, he argued, should not be rejected simply because of their form, antiquity or because composed by humans. Collins also issued a preemptive strike against one of the main reasons many Baptists might have been averse to the creeds—their link to the Roman Catholic Church. Collins avers that truth must be recognized wherever it may be found, even if mixed with error. This insightful statement by Collins reveals not only how he utilized the creeds, but may also reveal how he would read the church fathers, and even the Puritans with whom he might have significant disagreements.

Both the Heidelberg Catechism and its Baptist counterpart are desirous of affirming core elements of the historic catholic teaching of the Ancient Church, of which the central one is the Trinity.[24] Thus, matching the Heidelberg word for word, the *Orthodox Catechism* asks: "Into how many parts is this Creed divided?" The answer: "Into three: the first of the eternal Father, and our creation: the second, of the Son and our redemption: the third, of the Holy Ghost, and our sanctification."[25] In clear contrast to the heterodoxy expressed by Thomas Collier with regard to the Trinity, the *Orthodox Catechism* then asserted the biblical doctrine in these words,

---

[23] Collins, *An Orthodox Catechism*, "The Preface;" Renihan, *True Confessions*, 238.

[24] Collins actually included the Nicene Creed of 325—interestingly enough, not the Niceno-Constantinopolitan Creed of 381—and the Athanasian Creed at the close of his catechism: Collins, *An Orthodox Catechism*, 71-74; Renihan, *True Confessions*, 284-87. As noted above in n. 41, Collins was following the *Orthodox Creed* in this decision.

[25] Collins, *An Orthodox Catechism*, 9; Renihan, *True Confessions*, 244.

In Essence One, in Persons Three

Q. Seeing there is but one only substance of God, why namest thou those three, the Father, the Son, and the Holy Ghost?

A. Because God hath so manifested himself in his Word, that these three distinct persons are that one true everlasting God.[26]

Collins, thus, clearly affirmed the historic orthodox understanding of the Trinity as *tres Personae, una Substantia*. Although, as Harmon has noted, this continuity with the patristic tradition may not be due to a "conscious engagement with the patristic tradition as a source of religious authority," but rather reflects continuities "retained from the ecclesiastical bodies out of which the confessing Baptist communities came or by which they were influenced."[27] This means that Collins likely received his creedal commitments to the doctrines of the Trinity and the person of Christ, not directly from the patristic tradition, but rather through Reformed statements such as the Heidelberg Catechism and the Westminster Confession of Faith, along with the Thirty-Nine Articles of the Church of England. Nevertheless, the inclusion of the three creeds from the patristic era in the *Orthodox Creed* and *Orthodox Catechism* argues for a more direct influence, even though these creeds had likely been received by the Baptist community from their inclusion in the Thirty-Nine Articles.[28]

---

[26] Collins, *An Orthodox Catechism*, 9; Renihan, *True Confessions*, 244. Collins has added an "and" between "true" and "everlasting."

[27] Harmon, *Towards Baptist Catholicity*, 77.

[28] The language introducing the three creeds used in both article 38 of the *Orthodox Creed* and "The Preface" to the *Orthodox Catechism* is almost identical to the language of article 8 of the Thirty-Nine Articles. "The three Credes, Nicene Crede, Athanasian Crede, and that which is commonlye called the Apostles' Crede, ought throughlye to be receaued and beleaued: for they may be proued by moste certayne warrauntes of holye scripture." Philip Schaff, *The Creeds of Christendom, with a History and Critical Notes*, vol. 3, *The Evangelical Protestant Creeds, with Translations* (1931; repr., Grand Rapids: Baker Books, 2007), 3:492.

Patristic Theology

The patristic era is noted for hammering out the important theological formulations of Nicaeno-Constantinopolitan Trinitarianism and Chalcedonian Christology. All of orthodox Christianity is indebted to the meticulous work of the careful Christian theologians of the first four centuries of church history. The confessions of faith of the seventeenth-century Baptists clearly reflect this tradition, though they likely received this tradition through the Reformed confessions of their forbears and contemporaries. The *Second London Confession of Faith*, which Collins signed along with thirty-six other representatives of Particular Baptist churches in and around London, contained clear affirmations of these foundational doctrines including language that can be traced back to their classic formulations in the patristic era.

Nicaeno-Constantinopolitan Trinitarianism

Regarding the doctrine of the Trinity, the *Second London Confession* states a clear affirmation of Nicaeno-Constantinopolitan theology.

> In this divine and infinite Being there are three subsistences, the Father the Word (or Son) and Holy Spirit, of one substance, power, and Eternity, each having the whole Divine Essence, yet the Essence undivided, the Father is of none neither begotten nor proceeding, the Son is Eternally begotten of the Father, the holy Spirit proceeding from the Father and the Son, all infinite, without beginning, therefore but one God, who is not to be divided in nature and Being; but distinguished by several peculiar relative properties, and personal relations; which doctrine of the Trinity is the foundation of all our Communion with God, and comfortable dependence on him.[29]

---

[29] *A Confession Of Faith* (1677), 12; Lumpkin, *Baptist Confessions of Faith*, 253.

Although much of this language can be traced to the Westminster Confession and Savoy Declaration, there are some unique Baptist contributions.[30] For example, the *Second London Confession* added the following section to the language adapted from the Westminster and Savoy confessions: "all infinite, without beginning, therefore but one God, who is not to be divided in nature and Being; but distinguished by several peculiar relative properties, and personal relations." This selection came from the *First London Confession*, except the last phrase "and personal relations."[31] This observation indicates that while the Baptists were desirous to use the orthodox language of their paedobaptist contemporaries, they were nevertheless both capable and willing to strengthen the language where they deemed necessary. To this point, when describing the three distinct persons of the Trinity, the framers of the *Second London Confession* parted from their esteemed Reformed contemporaries to use the term "subsistence," a common English translation of *hypostasis*.[32] This no doubt reflects that, at the very least, these Baptists had a theological vocabulary that was informed by the Trinitarian debates of the patristic era. The use of "subsistence" also likely indicates that these Baptists were interested in specifically refuting the error of Thomas Collier who explicitly denied that God is "as some imagine, Three Persons yet one God, or three subsistings, distinguished though not divided."[33]

Collins' commitment to the classic formulation of the doctrine of the Trinity is not only seen in his approbation of the *Second London Confession* as one of its original signatories, he also positively asserted this doctrine in his *An Orthodox Catechism*. As noted

---

[30] For a comparison of the *Second London Confession* with its three primary source documents (Westminster Confession, Savoy Declaration, and *First London Confession*), see Renihan, *True Confessions*, 63–189.

[31] Cf. *First London Confession*, chapter II.

[32] Harmon, *Towards Baptist Catholicity*, 75, 75n15.

[33] Collier, *A General* Epistle, 4.

above, the *Orthodox Catechism* follows wholly the structure of the Heidelberg Catechism upon which it is based. The structure of the catechism is Trinitarian, with three sections focusing respectively upon the work of the Father, Son, and Holy Spirit. Collins explicitly states his commitment to the historic Christian doctrine by following the Heidelberg in including the following pointed catechetical question and response.

> Q. Seeing there is but one only substance of God, why namest thou those three, the Father, the Son, and the Holy Ghost?
>
> A. Because God hath so manifested himself in his Word, that these three distinct persons are that one true everlasting God.[34]

This statement affirms both of the key aspects of Trinitarian theology: the one substance or essence of God (*Substantia* or *Ousia*) and the three distinct persons (*Personae* or *Hypostases*) of the Father, Son, and Holy Spirit.

In Collins' other writings, a clear commitment to the doctrine of the Trinity is also seen. In his manual on preaching, *The Temple Repair'd*, Collins recommended to prospective preachers "Dr. Owen on the Trinity."[35] This was likely a reference to John Owen's *A Brief Declaration and Vindication of the Doctrine of the Trinity*, first published in 1669.[36] This is yet another indication that Collins would have seen himself as sharing the Trinitarian

---

[34] Collins, *An Orthodox Catechism*, 9; Renihan, *True Confessions*, 244. Collins has added an "and" between "true" and "everlasting."

[35] Hercules Collins, *The Temple Repair'd: Or, An Essay to revive the long-neglected Ordinances, of exercising the spiritual Gift of Prophecy for the Edification of the Churches; and of ordaining Ministers duly qualified* (London: William and Joseph Marshal, 1702), 49.

[36] John Owen, *A Brief Declaration and Vindication of the Doctrine of the Trinity* (London: R. W., 1669).

theology of his Reformed contemporaries. Additionally, Collins clearly assumed the Triune God in his epic poem tracing the story of redemptive history, *The Marrow of Gospel-History*.[37] In the opening scene, which begins in the throne room of God before the creation of the universe, Collins extolled the "Everliving God" as existing:

In all his Will immutable,
For Changes he knows none:
How can that be, when perfect's he,
Three Persons yet but One?[38]

This is a clear refutation of Collier's teaching, cited earlier, which explicitly stated that God is "not ... Three Persons yet one God."[39] Again, in poetic manner, Collins affirms the one essence and three persons of the Trinity.

Elsewhere, Collins provided insight into his own thinking on the Trinity in his illustration to prospective preachers of how one might draw doctrines from a particular passage of Scripture. The eighth doctrine which Collins drew from Colossians 1:12 was a Trinitarian observation:

That it is the Duty of all who are made meet for Heaven, to give Thanks to the Father. Mark one thing, tho it be said, that we should give Thanks to the Father, yet that doth not exclude the Son, nor the Holy Ghost, but it is to the Father as the Fountain of Grace, to the Son as the Procurer of Grace, to the Holy Spirit as the Applier of grace.[40]

---

[37] Hercules Collins, *The Marrow of Gospel-History: Or, A Diversion for Youth at their spare Hours* (London, 1696). Also published in Hercules Collins, *Three Books* (London, 1696).
[38] Collins, *The Marrow of Gospel-History*, 4.
[39] Collier, *A General Epistle*, 4.
[40] Collins, *The Temple Repair'd*, 49.

This reflection indicates that Collins was influenced by Puritan thinkers such as John Owen who often spoke of the Trinity in precisely these terms. In his magisterial work on Puritan theology, Joel R. Beeke has explained Owens' use of this terminology.

> Repeatedly Owen taught that there is a divine economy of operation where each person takes a role in the work of God, a role that reflects the personal relations in the Trinity. The Father acts as origin, authority, fountain, initiator, and sender; the Son acts as executor of the Father's will, treasury of His riches, foundation, worker, purchaser, and accomplisher; the Spirit acts as completer, finisher, immediate efficacy, fruit, and applier. This is not to divide God's works and distribute them among the three persons—the external works of the Trinity are undivided—but rather to recognize that in every work of God all three persons cooperate in distinct ways.[41]

Collins was clearly quite comfortable in expressing his orthodox convictions on the Trinity in terminology made familiar to him by his Puritan contemporaries. Although each member of the Godhead was considered as a distinct person, there was a unity of purpose and cooperation within the Trinity in the accomplishment of that purpose. Again, this was a truth earlier denied by Thomas Collier in the middle of the seventeenth century. Collier asserted that it was "altogether impossible to distinguish God in this manner, and not divide him; thus to distinguish is to divide; for three persons are three not only distinguished, but divided."[42] For Collier, to distinguish the persons of the Trinity in this way made three Gods and this could not be reconciled with the oneness of God. Collins' ruminations upon the Trinity, however, reflected

---

[41] Joel R. Beeke and Mark Jones, *A Puritan Theology: Doctrine for Life* (Grand Rapids: Reformation Heritage Books, 2012), 106.

[42] Collier, *A General Epistle*, 4.

not only the orthodoxy of the patristic period, but also the mature thought of the Puritan divines regarding the relationship between the one essence and three persons of God.

Chalcedonian Christology

As noted earlier in this essay, the *Second London Confession of Faith* was issued, in part, to set the record straight with the general public that Thomas Collier's heterodox views on the Trinity and the eternality of Christ's human nature did not represent the Particular Baptist community as a whole. The former has already been explored above. The latter is addressed in the confession's strong statement on the full divinity and humanity of Christ united in his one person.

> The *Son* of *God*, the second Person in the *Holy Trinity*, being very and eternal *God*, the brightness of the Fathers glory, of one substance and equal with *him*: who made the World, who upholdeth and governeth all things he hath made: did when the fullness of time was come take unto him mans nature, with all the Essential properties, and common infirmities thereof, yet without sin: being conceived by the *Holy Spirit* in the *Womb* of the *Virgin Mary*, the *Holy Spirit* coming down upon her, and the power of the most *High* overshadowing her, and so was made of a *Woman*, of the Tribe of *Judah*, of the Seed of *Abraham*, and *David* according to the *Scriptures*: So that two whole, perfect, and distinct natures, were inseparably joined together in one *Person*: without *conversion*, *composition*, or *confusion*: which *Person* is very *God*, and very *Man*, yet one *Christ*, the only *Mediator* between *God* and *Man*.[43]

Contra Collier's position on the eternality of Christ's human

---

[43] *A Confession Of Faith* (1677), 28–29; Lumpkin, *Baptist Confessions of Faith*, 260-61.

nature,[44] the confession asserts that Christ "did when the fullness of time was come take unto him man's nature, with all the Essential properties, and common infirmities thereof, yet without sin." The human nature was assumed at the incarnation and did not exist prior to this point in human history. At this point, the framers of the *Second London Confession* were following the wording found in the Westminster Confession and Savoy Declaration. Just after this section, however, the *Second London* adapts language from the *First London Confession* not included in either of these historic Protestant confessions. This wording further emphasized the full humanity assumed by the second person of the Trinity at Bethlehem. They added: "the *Holy Spirit* coming down upon her, and the power of the most *High* overshadowing her, and so was made of a *Woman*, of the Tribe of *Judah*, of the Seed of *Abraham*, and *David* according to the *Scriptures*."[45] This issue was important because these Baptists believed that the same human nature possessed by Eve, Judah, Abraham, and David was shared by the Christ. Only in this way could the prophecies concerning the Messiah's coming be fulfilled.

Collins highlighted another important reason for the real and full humanity of Christ in his *An Orthodox Catechism*. Namely, because "the Justice of God requireth that the same humane nature which hath sinned, do itself likewise make recompence for sin."[46] In order for God's justice to be satisfied, the same human nature which sinned had to make payment for sin. Thus, the Christ had to assume a human nature from his human mother, which had been passed down to her by her human ancestors. But one who is only fully human could not provide atonement for sin, for "he that

---

[44] Collier, *The Body of Divinity, Or, a Confession of Faith*, 31; Collier, *An Additional Word To The Body of Divinity*, 1-18.

[45] *A Confession of Faith* (1677), 29; Lumpkin, *Baptist Confessions of Faith*, 261; Renihan, *True Confessions*, 96.

[46] Collins, *An Orthodox Catechism*, 6; Renihan, *True Confessions*, 242.

is himself a sinner, cannot make recompence for others."[47] This required the deliverer of mankind to be a sinless human and one who has the power to "sustain in his flesh the burthen of God's wrath."[48] Collins follows the Heidelberg Catechism in asserting that this mediator must be fully God and fully human: "Such a one verily as is very man, and perfectly just, and yet in power above all creatures, that is, who is also very God."[49] This mediator is the Lord Jesus Christ who is "together both very God, and a very perfectly just man."[50] This view of the unity of the two natures in the person of Christ reflects the historic formulation of the Creed of Chalcedon of 451 which stated that Christ was

> to be acknowledged in two natures, *inconfusedly, unchangeably, indivisibly, inseparably*; the distinction of natures being by no means taken away by the union, but rather the property of each nature being preserved, and concurring in one Person and one Subsistence, not parted or divided into two persons, but one and the same Son, and only begotten, God the Word, the Lord Jesus Christ.[51]

This doctrine was affirmed by the *Second London Confession*'s declaration that in Christ "two whole, perfect, and distinct natures, were inseparably jointed together in one *Person*: without *conversion, composition*, or *confusion*: which *Person* is very *God*, and very *Man*; yet one *Christ*, the only *Mediator* between *God* and *Man*."[52]

Collins made clear his own personal commitment to this union of two natures in Christ in his own writings. Among his 36

---

[47] Collins, *An Orthodox Catechism*, 6; Renihan, *True Confessions*, 242.
[48] Collins, *An Orthodox Catechism*, 6; Renihan, *True Confessions*, 242.
[49] Collins, *An Orthodox Catechism*, 5; Renihan, *True Confessions*, 242.
[50] Collins, *An Orthodox Catechism*, 6; Renihan, *True Confessions*, 242.
[51] Philip Schaff, *The Creeds of Christendom, with a History and Critical Notes*, vol. 2, *The Greek and Latin Creeds, with Translations* (1931; repr., Grand Rapids: Baker Books, 2007), 2:62.
[52] *A Confession of Faith*, 29; Renihan, *True Confessions*, 96–97.

recommendations to preachers on how to rightly handle the Word of God in *The Temple Repair'd*, Collins included an explanation of how scriptural language often reflects this understanding of the union of the two natures.

> In holy Scripture you will sometimes find that which properly belongs to one Nature in Christ is attributed to another by virtue of the personal Union; hence it is that the Church is said to be *purchased with the blood of God*;[53] not that God simply consider'd hath Blood, *for he is a Spirit*;[54] but it is attributed to God, because of the Union of the Human and Divine Nature. Moreover, it is said that the *Son of Man was in Heaven*, when he was discoursing upon Earth:[55] Here that which was proper to the Godhead and the Divine Nature, is attributed to the Human Nature, because of the Union of the Natures.[56]

Here Collins' commitment to the hypostatic union becomes an important hermeneutical principle. He indicated the importance of explaining this in one's preaching "with all the clearness imaginable," because this doctrine "is so necessary to Man's Salvation."[57] For Collins and his fellow Particular Baptists, doctrine mattered. Indeed, the salvation of individuals depended upon the proper explication of the key doctrines of the Christian faith. Collins considered the doctrine of the hypostatic union of Christ's two natures to be at the very core of orthodox Christianity.[58] Humans need a savior who is simultaneously divine, human, and sinless. This is precisely the kind of savior which Collins saw set forth

---

[53] See Acts 20:28.
[54] See John 4:24.
[55] John 3:13.
[56] Collins, *The Temple Repair'd*, 38–39.
[57] Collins, *The Temple Repair'd*, 39.
[58] In *The Marrow of Gospel-History*, Collins extols the theological truth of the hypostatic union in poetic terms. See Collins, *The Marrow of Gospel-History*, 15, 18, and 93–94.

in Scripture. Ultimately, the never-ending union of the divine and human natures of Christ serve as an illustration of the eternal union between God and his elect because of the work of Christ. Collins expressed the security of the believer's union with Christ poetically in *The Marrow of Gospel-History*.

> That tho by Sin Man's separate
> From God, the chiefest Good,
> Yet now in Christ united are;
> Man shall live still with God.
> And if the Union cannot cease,
> Call'd *Hypostatical*;
> No more can that 'tween God and his,
> Because 'tis Eternal.[59]

Conclusion

Although admittedly difficult to comprehend fully, the doctrines of the Trinity and the person of Christ were not matters to be avoided by the seventeenth-century English Baptists. Rather, these doctrines were considered to be vital to orthodox Christianity. Both the General and Particular Baptist communities faced challenges to historic Nicaeno-Constantinopolitan Trinitarianism and Chalcedonian Christology. The General Baptist response to Matthew Caffyn is found in the *Orthodox Creed*. Particular Baptists also responded to the doctrinal deviations of Thomas Collier with a new confession, the *Second London Confession of Faith* in 1677. Hercules Collins, though an original signer of the *Second London Confession* at the General Assembly in 1689, also utilized the General Baptist's *Orthodox Creed* in the formation of his *Orthodox Catechism* in 1680. His commitment to the Christian orthodoxy of the patristic period is shown in his inclusion of three definitive creeds from the era. Furthermore, his writings are filled

---

[59] Collins, *The Marrow of Gospel-History*, 94.

with references that demonstrate both a familiarity with and a strong commitment to the classic definitions of the doctrines of the Trinity and the person of Christ hammered out in these early periods.

2
Scripture Demonstrations of the Holy Trinunity: Benjamin Keach's Defense of the Doctrine of the Trinity[1]

Jonathan W. Arnold

When Paul Best (1590-1657) and John Biddle (1615/16-1662) faced charges of blasphemy in the late 1640s, their hope for continued life—let alone for freedom—appeared bleak. Only three decades prior, the English crown had seen fit to execute two men, Batholomew Legate (d. 1612) and Edward Wightman (1580? - 1612), for publishing antitrinitarian tracts, the same precipitating events that had resulted in the incarceration of Best and Biddle. In the earlier version of this scenario, authorities had not only seen fit to execute the two heretics, but they had also gathered the offending documents—including all copies of the infamous primer of Socinian theology, the *Racovian Catechism*—and burned them in public, execution-style, in order to save England from the damnable heresies of Socinus and friends.

On paper, precious little differentiated the teachings associated with the earlier heretics from the teachings of the men incarcerated in the Gatehouse, Westminster in 1647. Both events led to charges of Socinianism, complete with its blatant dismissal of

---

[1] Much of the material for this article can be found with more detail in the author's work: Jonathan W. Arnold, *The Reformed Theology of Benjamin Keach (1640-1704)* (Oxford: Centre for Baptist History and Heritage, 2013), see especially, ch. 4. Material here has been used with the generous permission of the publisher.

trinitarian orthodoxy, and to convictions at the hands of the establishment. Unlike Legate and Wightman, however, Best and Biddle lived to see freedom beyond their incarceration. Additionally, in the immediate aftermath of the Best and Biddle trials, the *Racovian Catechism* arose from the flames and found a permanent place in the English literary landscape, safe from the fires that had consumed them previously. Even more telling, Biddle actually claimed to have developed his views on the Trinity independent of Socinus or his Bohemian followers. Enough changes had occurred in England for a uniquely English heterodox underground to develop.

The same cultural shifts in England that came to a head in the Biddle and Best test cases laid the foundation for the trinitarian discussions that took center stage amongst the dissenting community in the second half of the century. Doctrinal issues that had earlier been "extirpated" by James I carrying out "one of the principall parts of that duetie which appertaines vnto a Christian King,"[2] reappeared with a vengeance and begged for a response from the religious community still seeking a place in polite religious society. Standing outside the established church meant being the perennial target of heresy charges, necessitating an apologetic response that both distinguished the dissenting communities from the legitimate heretics—especially if the government was no longer willing to play the role of adjudicator—and anchored the orthodoxy of the various dissenting communities for both their own congregants and the public at large. Amongst the burgeoning sect of self-described "churches which are commonly (though falsly) called Anabaptists" and the "congregations of Christians (baptized upon Profession of their Faith),"[3] the task of defending

---

[2] *His Maiesties declaration concerning his proceedings with the States generall of the Vnited Prouinces of the Low Countreys, in the cause of D. Conradus Vorstius* (London: Robert Barker, 1612), 1.

[3] These are the titles from two early Baptist confessions of faith.

the doctrinal legitimacy fell to passionate clergy who not only guided their congregations during the tumultuous seventeenth century but also laid out the theological systems that would influence future generations of Baptist dissenters.

One of the most vocal of the second generation of those pastoral apologists, Benjamin Keach (1640–1704), found himself awash in the trinitarian debates that continued to thrive well into the 1700s. The theological heritage Keach claimed both for himself and for his congregation meeting on the southside of the River Thames had been involved in this particular debate since it first returned to English soil. Keach's own literary mentor, the illustrious Independent theologian, John Owen (1616–1683), attacked John Biddle's arguments in his 1655 publication, entitled *Vindiciae evangelicae or The mystery of the Gospell vindicated, and Socnianisme examined*. In that massive tome, Owen used nearly 700 pages to refute all of the major points of Biddle's version of Socinianism. That volume by Owen only piled onto the already-lengthy list of publications defending the historical doctrine of the trinity from the more acceptable dissenters as well as the establishment. Presbyterians like Matthew Poole, the dissenter known for his *Annotations upon the Bible*, and Church of England clergy like Nicolas Estwick (ca. 1584–1658) all saw fit to publish book-length responses to the increasingly-accepted anti-Trinitarianism of Biddle and Best.

When the major sects of English Protestantism saw fit to publish their confessional statements around the middle of the century, the article on the trinity, then, served as more than a merely perfunctory nod to classical creeds. In fact, both the *Savoy Declaration*, penned by the Independents, and the Baptist congregations' *Second London Confession* explicitly declared that the "doctrine of the Trinity is the foundation of all our Communion with

God, and comfortable dependence on him."[4] This specific acceptance of classical trinitarianism and the defensive posture of the "acceptable" versions of Christianity in seventeenth-century England in no way calmed the noisy discussions instigated by Biddle and Best; rather, they often made the work of the average dissenting pastor even more difficult. In fact, by the time Benjamin Keach explicitly joined the published discussion, the fight over trinitarianism had moved decidedly inside the bounds of acceptable religion. No longer were those who questioned the long-accepted position of the creeds seen as obvious heretics. Instead, new discussions arose from such ensconced theologians as William Sherlock (1639/40-1707), installed as Master of the Temple in London in 1685, and Stephen Nye (1648-1719), an outspoken Unitarian whose work on the history of the Unitarian movement ultimately led to the squelching of the debate by the Archbishop of Canterbury, Thomas Tenison (1636-1715).

Keach's Involvement

Despite coming of age at a time when Biddle and Best garnered nearly everyone's attention (Keach joined the General Baptist congregation meeting in Buckinghamshire in 1655 and began preaching in Aylesbury in 1658), Benjamin Keach did not directly involve himself in the trinitarian discussions until the last decade of the seventeenth century. Even then, his focus remained far more on the practical outworkings of the doctrine than on the often-pedantic discussions regarding terminology. This silence from Keach stemmed ostensibly from his understood calling as a pastor to laity—and to Baptist laity, at that—rather than to any ignorance on Keach's part. Throughout his writings, Keach demonstrated an active knowledge of the theological discussions that engulfed the academics of his day, and he rarely hesitated, in

---

[4] Savoy Declaration and *Second London Confession*, Article 2.

other debates, to engage even the most well-respected, well-educated theologians should the opportunity present itself. In the trinitarian debates, that opportunity never fully materialized.

Despite revealing himself to be well-versed in the contemporary trinitarian debates, Keach actually remained uncharacteristically aloof from the often-heated polemical discussions on this particular issue, not publishing a work focused directly on the topic until his work in 1700 entitled *Beams of divine light*. That publishing silence, however, did not render Keach's trinitarian writings any less pointed, nor did it indicate a lack of concern on his part. Rather, the relative quiet from Keach's pen could more aptly be attributed to Keach's view of the doctrine of the trinity as *the* foundation of all of his theological writings and, only secondarily, to the efficacy of the polemical works which had been published by those closest to him, including the work of a prominent church member, Isaac Marlow, who published his *A treatise of the Holy Trinunity* in 1690. Thus, the work required for modern readers to understand Keach's trinitarian theology proves to be more labor-intensive than comprehending, for instance, his views on baptism, sabbatarianism, or even eschatology given the number of polemical writings he published directly on those issues. That labor, however, does not come without rich rewards as Keach's trinitarianism—shaped in the midst of near-constant academic discussion—provides unique insights into the foundations of trinitarian theology for successive generations of Baptists.

Keach's Trinitarian System

Unsurprisingly, from his earliest forays into public ministry, Keach organized his theological teaching around a trinitarian structure in use since the earliest days of the church. The first of his published works, a children's primer that—due to its anti-paedobaptist teachings and perceived radical eschatology—had been burned at the order of Judge Robert Hyde in 1664, almost certainly included the confession of faith that appeared at the end of the version he reportedly reproduced from memory in 1695. That work, like the Nicene-Constantinopolitan Creed or the Apostles' Creed, centered around several "I believe" statements aligned in a clearly trinitarian fashion.

> I believe with my Heart, and Confess with my Mouth, That God is one Almighty, Eternal, Infinite and admirable Essence ... I also believe in Jesus Christ our Lord, who is the only begotten Son of God, being the brightness of his Glory, and express Image of his Person, and he is verily God of the substance of the Father; so he is truly Man ... I also believe in the Holy Ghost, who is one with the Father & Son, proceeding from them ... I believe also, God hath a holy and blessed Church on Earth, who are a select People, separated from the evil customs and worships of the World according to Gods Holy Word. I also believe the Resurrection of the Dead, the Eternal Judgment, with the Life everlasting, Amen.[5]

Consequently, Keach made clear from the earliest stage of his career that he stood firmly in the trinitarian camp. By identifying Jesus Christ as "the only begotten Son of God" who is "verily God of the substance of the Father" and "the Holy Ghost, who is one with the Father & Son," Keach distinguished his brand of theology from any number of dissenting groups, including the group of Baptists who signed the so-called *Standard Confession* in 1660. That confession—signed by, among others, Joseph Keach, Benjamin's brother—notably did not contain explicit trinitarian language save for the direct quotation of the already-controversial *Comma Johanneum* (1 John 5:7).

---

[5] Benjamin Keach, *The child's delight: or instructions for children and youth. Wherein all the chief principles of the Christian religions are clearly (though briefly) opened*, 3rd corrected ed. (London: William and Joseph Marshall, 1704), 50–51.

Jonathan W. Arnold

Extra-biblical Terminology

The signers of the *Standard Confession* almost certainly avoided much of the common trinitarian language primarily due to a deep-seated reticence toward any use of extra-biblical language to describe God. That reticence led to a strange consortium of cobelligerents, reaching far beyond the signatories of that document and consisting of traditional trinitarians and radical anti-Trinitarians connected by their mutual opposition to such language. Thus, such disparate theologians as Thomas Grantham (1634–1692), the eminent General Baptist messenger and traditional trinitarian, and Matthew Tindal (1657–1733), the early English deist and defender of Unitarianism, could agree that the use of extrabiblical terminology caused more problems than solutions. As Grantham argued, "It is not necessary to impose words upon any Man which God himself hath not used, by which to make himself known."[6] Tindal was more forceful: "[t]o prefer Tradition before our clearest idea's [in biblical revelation]," he argued, "is to prefer probably before certain, Belief before Knowledg, that which we possibly may be mistaken in, before what we are most certain of."[7]

Those arguments held no sway for Keach, who not only eschewed that reticence in his works intended for his broader readership but also ensured that his own congregation would align with the traditional language by including it in his church's confessional statement. According to that statement of faith, published in 1697, "there are three Persons in the Godhead, the *Father*, the *Son*, and *Holy Spirit*; and that *these three are One God*, the

---

[6] Thomas *Grantham, Christianismus primitivus; or, The ancient Christian religion*, Book 2, part 1 (London, 1678), 40.

[7] Matthew Tindal, *A letter to the reverend the clergy of both universities, concerning the Trinity and the Athanasian creed with reflections on all the late hypotheses, particularly Dr. W's, Dr. S—th's, the Trinity placed in its due light, The 28 propositions, The calm discourse of a Trinity in the Godhead, and the defence of Dr. Sherlock's notions: with a short discourse concerning mysteries* (London, 1694), 34.

same in Essence, equal in Power and Glory."[8] Given his interaction with William Sherlock and Robert South and his close connection to John Owen and Isaac Chauncy (1632-1712)—all of whom had been involved in the trinitarian debates which centered on the semantic usage of terms like *person* and *essence*—Keach's use of these terms could hardly be seen as coincidental.

Use of Tradition

The debate around trinitarian terminology also called into question the relationship of the church to tradition as a whole. Those who shied away from the use of extra-biblical terminology did so consistently on the basis of an extreme biblicism that had come into vogue in England alongside the development of a native English anti-Trinitarianism. Paul Best, for example, grounded his own anti-Trinitarianism in the simple fact that "for the Son to be coequall to the Father, or the holy Spirit a distinct coequall person I cannot finde [in Scripture]."[9] According to that view, expressed accurately in the *Racovian Catechism*, an individual should reject "every interpretation [of Scripture] which is repugnant to right reason."[10] This emphasis on reason meant being willing to discard the interpretations of the past, the "historical writings, or other authentic testimonies and sources of information"[11] should they be deemed to be in opposition to the Bible as interpreted by right reason.

For Keach, this pervasive Socinian understanding of tradition and even the Bible as subservient to reason stood against historic

---

[8] Benjamin Keach, *The articles of the faith of the Church of Christ, or, Congregation meeting at Horsley-down* (London, 1697).

[9] Paul Best, *Mysteries discovered. Or, A mercuriall picture pointing out the way from Babylon to the Holy city, for the good of all such as ... have been so long misled with Romes hobgoblins* (London, 1647), 5.

[10] Thomas Rees, *The Racovian catechism, with notes and illustrations, translated from the Latin: to which is prefixed a sketch of the history of Unitarianism in Poland and the adjacent countries* (London: Longman, Hurst, Rees, Orme, and Brown, 1818), 18.

[11] Rees, *Racovian catechism*, 16.

Christianity. In response, Keach enumerated a clear hierarchy of authority which he utilized throughout his many theological writings, including those focused on the doctrine of the trinity.[12] Unsurprisingly, the first level of that hierarchy—the argument from "the Word of God"—provided Keach with the most fodder for his doctrinal writings. After all, he, like the Reformers he willingly followed, viewed "the holy Scriptures as a sufficient Rule in all points of Faith and Practice."[13] Without fail, Keach turned to the Bible first and repeatedly for his arguments. He also berated those of his opponents who did not see the obvious arguments from Scripture. To ignore the clear reading of Scripture in favor of tradition meant succumbing to nothing more than "humane" arguments—one of the many shortcomings of the popish religion and various other sects. Keach, indeed, celebrated those of his audience who did "not ma[k]e Men, General Councils, nor Synods, your Rule, but God's Holy Word: your Constitution, Faith, and Discipline."[14] Moreover, Keach did not limit his understanding of the clear meaning of Scripture simply to the literal words of the text; rather, he argued: "That which by a just and necessary Consequence is deduced from Scripture, is as much the Mind of Christ, as what is contained in the express words of Scripture."[15]

This understanding allowed Keach to harmonize his high view of the authority of Scripture with his argument for the use of "Universal Tradition" and "the Testimony of most approved Writers"—the second and third levels of his hierarchy,

---

[12] Benjamin Keach, *The Jewish sabbath abrogated, or, The Saturday sabbatarians confuted,* sermons (London, 1700), 186.

[13] Benjamin Keach, *Christ alone the way to Heaven: or, Jacob's ladder improved,* 4 sermons. *To which is added, one sermon on Rom. 8. 1. With reflections on S. Clark's Scripture justification* (London, 1698), 10.

[14] Benjamin Keach, *The breach repaired in God's worship, or, Singing of psalms, hymns, and spiritual songs, proved to be an holy ordinance of Jesus Christ with an answer to all objections* (London: John Hancock, 1691), iii-iv.

[15] Benjamin Keach, *The rector rectified and corrected; or, infant-baptism unlawful* (London: John Harris, 1692), 33.

respectively. Those latter terms had distinctive meanings in Keach's system. The "Universal Tradition," or "Apostolical Tradition,"[16] referred to the doctrines of the church as established by the earliest councils and accepted by all branches of Christendom. The final level of his hierarchical system allowed Keach to place himself in a broader contemporary conversation without losing sight of the biblical theology that he believed should be the focus. Those "most approved Writers," for Keach, included his favorite theologian, John Owen, Owen's successor at the Independent Church meeting at Bury-Street, Isaac Chauncy, any number of baptist pastor-theologians, and those leaders of the Reformation who defend the "Orthodoxy of Matter."[17] In enumerating this structure, Keach clearly intended to aid his readers as they navigated the complex and ever-changing theological discussions of their day. For Keach's theological stance, this method allowed him to hold a high view of Scripture in tension with a respect for historic Christianity and to engage the contemporary debates without losing sight of the final objective, namely, to understand God as He "hath revealed or made known himself"[18] in Scripture.

The Doctrine
Despite his inherent respect for human reason and the Christian tradition, Keach's ultimate understanding of the Triunity of the Godhead fell into a category of divine mystery which could only

---

[16] Benjamin Keach, *Pedo-baptism disproved being an answer to two printed papers .... The second edition: to which is added twenty sylogistical arguments to disprove infant-baptism. ed* (London: John Harris, 1691), 23.

[17] Thomas De Laune and Benjamin Keach, *Tropologia, or, A key to open Scripture metaphors*, Book II: sig. A3r (London: Enoch Prosser), *1681*).

[18] Benjamin *Keach, A golden mine opened, or, The glory of God's rich grace displayed in the mediator to believers and his direful wrath against impenitent sinners containing the substance of near forty sermons upon several subjects* (London: William Marshall, 1694), 91.

be accepted by faith.[19] Any accurate concept of the Godhead could only come via divine revelation of the three Persons, specifically "their properties and operations [rather than] by their essential forms ... which are in themselves absolutely incomprehensible."[20] Keach, then, attempted to describe the three Persons according to their unique, individual tasks, but he remained firm in his understanding of the essential union of the Triune God. That understanding, after all, involved a God who "though three Persons or Subsistences, yet [was] but one and the same God, one in Essence, though distinguished as to their distinct Personalities."[21] While Keach did not often write exclusively on the doctrine of the Trinity, he did touch on the connected issues throughout his writings. His teaching on salvation, for example, proved to be quite fruitful for Keach to introduce his audience to the contemporary debates on the topic. Two of his collections of sermons in particular provide helpful insights into his understanding of the significance of the doctrine of the trinity as a foundation for salvation. Both of those collections—*A golden mine opened* (1694) and *Gospel mysteries unveil'd* (1701)—were published in the last decade of his ministry during a time when the debates over trinitarianism had grown increasingly heated.

In a sermon entitled "The Glory of the Lord Revealed," Keach took the opportunity afforded by the quotation of Isaiah found in Luke 3 to explore the glory-revealing aspect of the divine work of salvation. According to his exposition, the Father served as the "first in order, in all the Divine Operations."[22] This

---

[19] Benjamin Keach, *The French impostour detected Or Zach. Housel, tryed the second time by the word of God* (London: Ebenezer Trasy, 1702), 141.

[20] De Laune and Keach, *Tropologia*, III:22.

[21] Keach, *A golden mine opened*, 377.

[22] Benjamin Keach, *Gospel mysteries unveil'd: or, An exposition of all the parables, and many express similitudes contained in the Four Evangelists spoken by our Lord and Saviour Jesus Christ: wherein also many things are doctrinally handled and practically improved by way of application* (London: R. Tookey, 1701), I:32.

understanding, combined with the modified form of the satisfaction theory of the atonement which Keach found to be both biblical and helpful, led Keach to teach that "[t]he Father was [the divine Person who was] injured, His glory seemed to be eclipsed by Sin."[23] The Father acted in choosing and sending the Son into the world, raised the Son from the dead, justified him and "us in him," and secured union for the believer in the Son.[24] Thus, Keach could argue, as he did in a sermon on Hebrews 2:3, that the Father functions as "the Fountain and Spring of [our great Salvation]."[25]

Keach understood quite well the potential pitfalls associated with this understanding of the First Person of the Trinity. By seeing the Father as the injured upholder of justice, some, including the Socinians, held that this teaching rendered "the Son more merciful and kind than the Father."[26] Because of both the co-essential nature of the three Persons as well as the fact that the Father could rightly be seen as the "Contriver or first Author of this Salvation,"[27] Keach dismissed these concerns as nothing more than "absurd Notion[s]"[28] made by those who did not understand either the nature of the Triune God or the outworking of salvation. According to the biblical account, "[a]ll the Blessings of our Salvation are ascribed to the free Bounty, Mercy, Love and Goodness of God the Father."[29] Even more, Keach argued that the Father's justice did not necessitate the relinquishing of his mercy. The unique glory of the salvific plan came in the fact that the Father could indeed be "Just as well as Gracious."[30]

---

[23] Keach, *A golden mine opened*, 377.
[24] Keach, *Gospel mysteries unveil'd*, I:32.
[25] Keach, *A golden mine opened*, 377.
[26] Keach cited "the Socinians" and William Penn (1644–1718), the early Quaker defender on both sides of the Atlantic. See Keach, *A golden mine opened*, 378.
[27] Keach, *A golden mine opened*, 377.
[28] Keach, *A golden mine opened*, 378.
[29] Keach, *A golden mine opened*, 378.
[30] Keach, *A golden mine opened*, 379.

Jonathan W. Arnold

At the most basic level, Keach's understanding of the Second Person of the Trinity closely followed his teaching on the Father. Whereas the Father's glory was bestowed in his orchestration of the work of salvation, the Son's glory was revealed in the actual carrying out of the plan. The "Exercis[ing] of his Offices ... when he was actually anointed and proclaimed *King, Priest* and *Prophet*" and his "obedience to the Law ... and ... his Death, glorious Resurrection and Ascension into Heaven" all combined to demonstrate both his essential divinity and his unity with the Father.[31]

In fact, none of Keach's teachings specifically on Christ would have surprised anyone who held to a classic view of the Godhead. He actively defended the basic teachings of Christendom: the divinity of Christ, the humanity of Jesus, and even the hypostatic union as defined by the Council of Chalcedon.[32] According to his view, Jesus Christ revealed himself as "the Eternal God; not God by Office, but God by Nature, the most High God who made Heaven and Earth, and yet truly Man, taking our Nature into a mystical Union with his Holy Deity ... and thus both God and Man in one Person."[33]

Discussions surrounding the Second Person of the Trinity commanded a larger portion of Keach's published works, especially as his readership struggled with the teachings of the General Baptist messenger, Matthew Caffyn (d. 1714), whose espousal of something akin to a celestial flesh view of Christ led to Keach labeling him as a "Destable [sic] and *Damnable*,"[34] "*rank*

---

[31] Keach, *Gospel mysteries unveil'd*, I:32.
[32] Keach actually used the term in at least five different works, and, in several additional works, he defined the concept of Christ's human and divine natures being united.
[33] Keach, *A golden mine opened*, 93.
[34] Benjamin Keach, *Beams of divine light: or Some brief hints of the being and attributes of God and of the three persons in the God-Head* (London: K. Allwood, 1700), 23.

Heretick."[35] Caffyn's teachings, though uniquely associated with the still-developing Baptist associations in the British Isles, were not unique in their attacks on this historic doctrine. Both Socinianism and Arianism presented their own unorthodox views of the Second Person of the Trinity as did the Quakers who were quickly gaining popularity in the English world and who had claimed one of Keach's own daughters, Hannah, as a convert.[36] Thus, Keach presented his apology of the Reformed orthodox view of Christ from a distinctly personal position. His writings on the subject provided a clear demonstration of that personal involvement, with his most passionate condemnations being reserved for those who questioned this historical view of Christ.

The doctrine of the Holy Spirit garnered nearly the same opposition from the anti-Trinitarians as the doctrine of the Son. The debate once again involved the usual suspects with the Socinians, on the one side, referring to the Spirit simply as "virtue or energy"[37] and the Quakers, on the other side, arguing that the Spirit is "the Light Within" or "Christ within."[38] Both of those anti-trinitarian attacks presented the Holy Spirit as something less than a distinct, divine Person of the Godhead.

For Keach, then, a defense of the Trinity required a robust explanation of a biblical pneumatology, whereby the Spirit could be rightly seen as "the voluntary Author of all Divine Operations" and is the divine Person who "*inlightneth, reneweth, regenerates, sanctifieth, teacheth and guideth.*"[39]

---

[35] Benjamin Keach, *The display of glorious grace: or, The covenant of peace opened* (London, 1698), 136.

[36] Thomas Crosby, *The history of the English baptists, from the Reformation to the beginning of the reign of King George I* (London, 1738), IV:308–309.

[37] Rees, *Racovian catechism*, 39.

[38] William Penn, *A discourse of the general rule of faith and practice, and judge of controversie* (London, 1699).

[39] Keach, *Gospel mysteries unveil'd*, I:32.

Jonathan W. Arnold

In other words, the Father orchestrates, the Son achieves, and the Spirit applies the work of salvation. By enumerating the unique roles of the Spirit, Keach provided a full-fledged discussion of his understanding of sanctification, or "union with Christ."[40] This particular discussion had far-reaching implications for Keach's theology, directly affecting his definition of the church—which he limited in its visible sense to baptized believers duly received into a local congregation, his identification of the ordinances and their roles—which he noted included the usual baptism and Lord's Supper but also included (at some points in his writings) the practice of laying on of hands of new believers,[41] and his understanding of assurance for the believer who could be absolutely certain that the Spirit would neither desert Christ nor the believer, thus rendering the Union unbreakable. In each of those areas, the Spirit played the central role of divine activity. The very idea that the Spirit could be viewed as anything less than a distinct, consubstantial Third Person of the Triune Godhead made no sense to Keach's understanding of Scripture and of historic Christianity.

Despite spending significant time and space describing the unique roles performed by each of the divine Persons, Keach, in the end, felt compelled to remind his audience of the mystery shrouding the Triunity of the God of the Bible. Keach recognized the value of the hierarchical system he enumerated for his audience: namely, when it was correctly applied, it protected the unsuspecting believer from the various pitfalls of theological heterodoxy that plagued the English landscape. More importantly for Keach, that theological hermeneutic led to nowhere other than the classical understanding of the Trinity as expressed by the great

---

[40] Benjamin Keach, *The ax laid to the root: or, One blow more at the foundation of infant baptism, and Church-membership* (London, 1693), 13.

[41] Benjamin Keach, *The articles of the faith of the Church of Christ, or, Congregation meeting at Horsley-down* (London, 1697), Article XXIII.

theologians of generations past, by Keach's compatriots who stood against the antitrinitarian upstarts, and by Keach himself. But Keach also recognized the inherent limitations of any human system, and he regularly highlighted those limitations even as he pointed his audience to God's Triunity. Even as he preached on the subject, he implored his hearers to remember "that it's beyond our Capacities fully to comprehend [the Trinity]."[42] Even still, he argued that from the totality of the biblical record and from the full corpus of his own work (and that of so many other worthy divines), "there are ... clear Scripture-Demonstrations, that in the Deity there is a plurality of distinct Persons, which might further be evinced, as the Learned have shown."[43] Thus, Keach could enjoin his congregation to sing about the mysterious truths that reached beyond human comprehension, whether that truth focused on Scripture itself and what it taught:

The sacred Scriptures are *sublime*,
Although *mysterious* be;
Their Matter shews they are divine,
Nay, their divinity

Is seen by what they do treat of,
Or unto us make known,
There we do read of great *Jehovah*,
The *high* and *lofty One*,

Of his dread *Essence*, nature pure,
And of the *Unity*
Between the *Father, Son,* and *Spirit*,
Or *holy Trinity*.[44]

---

[42] Keach, *A golden mine opened*, 92.
[43] Keach, *A golden mine opened*, 92.
[44] Benjamin Keach, *Spiritual melody, containing near three hundred hymns* (London, 1691), 224.

Jonathan W. Arnold

or more directly focused on the very nature of God:

> Thou art afar, yet always near;
> Immoveable, yet ev'ry where,
> Eternally the same:
> Thy Nature's Light, thy Nature's Love;
> Thou dwell'st below, thou dwell'st above;
>   All glorious is thy Name.
>
> Thou art a glorious Mystery,
> In Essence One, in Persons Three,
>   Eternal and divine:
> By Saints and Angels high ador'd,
>   All Praise and Glory's thine.[45]

Outcomes

By the time Keach's ministry reached its zenith in the last decade of the seventeenth century, William III intervened in the trinitarian debates, issuing a royal injunction in 1696. Parliament followed suit with the Blasphemy Act of 1697, in their attempt to quell the groundswell of anti-Trinitarianism that had become commonplace since Biddle and Best had successfully avoided execution a half-century earlier. Keach rightly saw that effort on the part of the establishment as too little and too late to serve as a legitimate defense of the doctrine that was foundational to every aspect of Christianity. Nearly all of his writings attacked, in one form or another, the increasingly acceptable forms of unorthodoxy. In that endeavor, he strived to deliver what he hoped was a clear, concise explanation of this key aspect of "the Essentials of Christ's

---

[45] Benjamin Keach, *War with the devil; or the young man's conflict with the powers of darkness; displayed in a poetical dialogue between youth and conscience* (Coventry: T. Luckman, n.d.), 107.

Doctrine of the Principles of true Religion."⁴⁶ As he did so, Keach demonstrated his capabilities as a pastor-theologian, his awareness of the theological struggles common to his audience, and his passion for what he perceived to be matters of Reformed orthodoxy. Ultimately, he laid an auspicious groundwork for the discussions that would arise in successive generations as trinitarianism continued to command the spotlight of English dissent.

---

⁴⁶ Keach, *A golden mine opened*, 85.

3
The Salters' Hall Controversy: Heresy, Subscription, or Both?

Jesse F. Owens

In February 1719, over one hundred dissenting ministers gathered at Salters' Hall in London to determine how they might advise the Presbyterians in Exeter who were concerned that their ministers held heterodox views on the doctrine of the Trinity.[1] The meeting at Salters' Hall, consisting of Presbyterians, Independents, and Baptists, was convened in order to help solve the controversy. But the Salters' Hall meetings became a separate controversy as the ministers in London were divided on how to respond to the issue in Exeter. Their division did not fall solely along denominational lines. The Baptists, Presbyterians, and Independents were divided on this: whether or not ministers ought to be required to subscribe to extrabiblical words and phrases delineating the doctrine of the Trinity, particularly when a minister's orthodoxy might be in doubt. Fifty-seven of the ministers there were opposed to requiring subscription. Fifty-three ministers were in favor of this requirement, and of recommending it to those in Exeter. The two parties, who became known as "Subscribers" and "Nonsubscribers," sent two separate sets of advices to Exeter.[2] Neither group's advice had any influence in Exeter, as they arrived after a decision

---

[1] The request for advice came from "the thirteen" but it is also surmised that James Peirce may have also appealed to John Shute Barrington for help in the matter.

[2] By the time that the advices were sent to Exeter, the number of Subscribers had grown to seventy-eight and the number of Nonsubscribers had grown to seventy-three.

had already been made to remove the pastors in question there.³ A pamphlet war quickly ensued as members of each party sought to not only declare their orthodoxy, but also to provide their account and interpretation of what had occurred at Salters' Hall.

A simple survey of the primary source material that came out of the Salters' Hall Controversy reveals that as early as 1719 there were disagreements on how to interpret the events. Was the issue at hand subscription to extrabiblical words and phrases? Or, was opposition to subscription a thinly veiled disguise for anti-Trinitarianism? These are the questions that this chapter seeks to answer. In order to answer them there are several items that must be taken into account. First, we need a better understanding of what occurred at Exeter since it was the controversy at Exeter that precipitated the controversy in London. Second, we need to briefly recount the proceedings at Salters' Hall before interpreting them. This includes understanding the political setting just prior to 1719. Third, we must take into consideration some of the earliest accounts of Salters' Hall, particularly the accounts of the revered ministers Edmund Calamy, a Presbyterian who abstained from the controversy, and Edward Wallin, a Particular Baptist Subscriber at Salters' Hall. Fourth, it must be noted that there is an orthodox, nonsubscribing tradition among the English General Baptists and the English Presbyterians connected to Thomas Grantham and Richard Baxter respectively. In the end, we can reasonably conclude that even if there were a few anti-Trinitarians among the Nonsubscribers at Salters' Hall, many were opposed to the additional requirement of subscription to extrabiblical words and phrases—not the doctrine of the Trinity.⁴

---

³ Their advices likely would not have had much influence even if they had arrived on time since the Exeter Presbyterians were appalled by the involvement of "Anabaptists" at the Salters' Hall meetings.

⁴ Another important question that should be considered in more detail is whether or not the London ministers, particularly for the General Baptists, are representative of General Baptist sentiments throughout England. Or, have the actions and

Jesse F. Owens

James Peirce, Joseph Hallet, and Exeter

By his own account, James Peirce held a classical understanding of the doctrine of the Trinity until sometime around 1713.[5] In retrospect, Peirce believed that he had been "bred up in a scheme, of which I can now make nothing else but *Sabellianism*."[6] When Peirce first heard about the writings of William Whiston and Samuel Clarke, he avoided reading them, but discussion of them was "very much increasing" until he encountered a friend who "reproach'd" him for his "sloth."[7] So Peirce purchased Clarke's *Scripture-doctrine* and Whiston's works and began to read them. He was mesmerized by Clarke's method of scripture citation, and finally "saw clearly" that he "must depart with some beloved opinions, or else quit" his "notion of the authority of the holy scriptures."[8] Peirce committed to read the Bible more carefully, and concluded that the classical doctrine of the Trinity was not taught clearly enough in the Bible to be made "a fundamental article of the Christian faith."[9]

Peirce soon became concerned about some practical matters related to his new beliefs. If he rejected the consubstantial Trinity, or at least did not think it expressly taught in Scripture, then his prayer and his preaching must be altered as well. Peirce's solution

---

sentiments of a few General Baptist ministers in and around London been unfairly viewed as representative of the whole? Paul Copson is helpful on this point. See Paul Copson, "Stogdon, Foster, and Bulkeley: Variations on an Eighteenth-Century Theme" in *Pulpit and People: Studies in Eighteenth-Century Baptist Life and Thought*, ed. John H. Y. Briggs (Eugene, OR: Wipf and Stock, 2009), 56. This same critique could potentially be leveled against the use of the Caffyn Controversy to discredit the General Baptists as being wholly inclined towards heterodoxy. Clint Bass' writings offers a moderating view on the subject. See Clint C. Bass, *Thomas Grantham (1633-1692) and General Baptist Theology* (Oxford, UK: Regent's Park College, 2013), 179-213.

[5] Peirce, *Western Inquisition*, 10.
[6] Peirce, *Western Inquisition*, 5.
[7] Peirce, *Western Inquisition*, 8.
[8] Peirce, *Western Inquisition*.
[9] Peirce, *Western Inquisition*, 9.

was to resort almost exclusively to scriptural words.[10] This led Peirce to eliminate the doxology he had formerly used at the end of his prayers. Of course, this all came to a head in time after Peirce was unanimously chosen to serve three dissenting congregations in Exeter in 1713. By the time that Peirce accepted this position, he had already ceased using the doxology in prayer and had become "throughly convinc'd that the common doctrine was not according to the scriptures."[11] Consequently, according to Peirce, he never used the doxology in his prayers at Exeter and committed to only speak of the doctrine of the Trinity in scriptural terms.

The controversy at Exeter began, however, in 1716 when concerns arose over Hubert Stogdon's theology of the Trinity. Stogdon had been educated in Exeter at Joseph Hallet's academy.[12] In November 1716, Stogdon openly confessed to John Lavington, the youngest minister in Exeter, that he had come to affirm Samuel Clarke's "new scheme" of the doctrine of the Trinity.[13] Clarke's scheme had come to prominence in 1712 with the publication of *The Scripture-doctrine of the Trinity*, which led many to reexamine whether or not the consubstantial Trinity was a biblical concept. As Clarke explored the biblical basis for the doctrine of the Trinity, William Whiston sought to demonstrate that the doctrine of the Trinity, as it had been expressed by the end of the fourth century, was largely the creative work of Athanasius. Whiston's works *Athanasius Convicted of Forgery* (1712) and *Primitive Christianity Reviv'd* (1712) appeared in print the same year as Clarke's seminal work, and their influence had been noted in Exeter. One Exeter citizen wrote: "Upon the coming out of Mr. *Whiston's* Books, these new Notions about the *Trinity*, were toss'd

---

[10] Peirce, *Western Inquisition*.

[11] Peirce, *Western Inquisition*, 10.

[12] Allan Brockett, *Non-Conformity in Exeter 1650–1875* (Manchester, UK: Manchester University Press, 1962), 80.

[13] Brockett, *Non-Conformity*, 80.

about by Mr. *Hallet's* Academicks, with too much Fondness."[14] The people of Exeter were convinced that Hallet's academy was to blame for the spread of heterodoxy there.[15]

Joseph Hallet and James Peirce came under suspicion for heterodoxy as well. Peirce and Hallet, apparently aware of Stogdon's heterodox views, sent him off to a neighboring county with a letter of recommendation for his ordination to the ministry. The letter was dated July 15, 1717, and it included the name of John Withers who was also a minister in Exeter. Their recommendation for Stogdon's ordination was a source of great tension between Hallet, Peirce, Withers, and many of their congregants. Another source of consternation was Peirce's refusal to include the doxology giving "Glory to the Father, Son, and Holy Ghost as One God" at "the close of the Psalm or Hymn." Peirce refused to continue this practice, believing that it was unscriptural.[16] The cumulative effect being that many of the citizens of Exeter began to not only be concerned about the spread of heterodoxy among their youth, but they also began to question the orthodoxy of their ministers.

By January 1718, a standing "Committee of Thirteen" along with a few other citizens of Exeter went to their ministers and requested that they defend the deity of Christ in a sermon.[17] In September 1718, at an assembly of the United Ministers of Devon and

---

[14] *Account of the Reasons*, 4.

[15] It should also be noted that those who embraced the new scheme "began to boast of their *Numbers*, and of their *Strength* among the *Ministers*, even defying the Assembly to take Cognizance of it." *Account of the Reasons*, 5.

[16] *Account of the Reasons*, 6.

[17] *Account of the Reasons*, 5. The Committee of Thirteen consisted of: James White, Samuel Munckly, Benjamin Brinley, Francis Lydston, Henry Walrond, Anthony Vicary, John Stephens, Edmond Cock, Mark Burridg, Thomas Jeffery, John Vowler, John Pym, and Jerome King. See *A Plain and Faithful Narrative of the Differences among the Dissenters at Exeter Relating to the Doctrine of the Ever Blessed Trinity, So far as gave Concern to some of the London Ministers* (London, 1719), 22-23. Jerome King is not listed in a *A Plain and Faithful Narrative*, according to Brockett, because he had recently died. See Brockett, *Non-Conformity*, 89.

Cornwall, each of the ministers present stood and professed their belief in the doctrine of the Trinity in their own words. It was the "General Sence of the *Assembly, That there is but One God; and that the Father, word and Holy Spirit is that One* God."[18] Yet, as Brockett explains, "Peirce openly declared his belief in the subordination of Son and Holy Ghost to God the Father, the first time he had done this in public."[19] The Committee of Thirteen met with Hallet, Lavington, Peirce, and Withers in November 1718 in order to ascertain their beliefs on the doctrine of the Trinity. The ministers were asked to affirm either the "general sense" of the previous assembly meeting, the answer to the fifth and sixth questions of the Westminster Shorter Catechism, or the first article of the Church of England. The Committee of Thirteen noted: "But we had no satisfaction to either of the said Proposals from three of our four Ministers; but instead thereof one of them expressly declared for a Subordination."[20] Almost certainly, Lavington had complied while Hallet, Peirce, and Withers did not.[21] Peirce likely was the one who openly declared his belief in the subordination of the Son and the Spirit.

A neighboring minister, John Walrond of Ottery, had sent a letter to William Tong, pastor at Salters' Hall, in the summer of 1718. In the letter he expressed his concern about the spread of Arianism at Exeter. The Committee of Thirteen, having made their concerns known to several neighboring ministers, including Walrond, would eventually appeal to some of the ministers in London themselves. But Walrond's letter is important because in it Walrond not

---

[18] *Account of the Reasons*, 5; Brockett, *Non-Conformity*, 87.

[19] Brockett, *Non-Conformity*, 87. It is somewhat unclear whether this occurred at the assembly meeting in September, or at a later meeting between Peirce and the Committee of Thirteen in November, 1718. *An Account of the Reasons* seems to state the latter. See *An Account of the Reasons*, 6.

[20] *A Plain and Faithful Narrative*, 21-2.

[21] Withers later affirmed the doctrine of the Trinity. See Brockett, *Non-Conformity*, 93.

only conveys his concerns about Exeter, but also states that it is his understanding that Arianism has spread among the London ministers as well.[22] Tong thought the contents of the letter so important that he gathered twenty-five ministers to meet at Salters' Hall to discuss the letter and draft a response. Their response, which was premised upon how they would respond "if ever we should be called that ungrateful Task," included five recommendations. First, "not to suspect any among us to be infected with these Errors unless we have good Ground." Second, "not to be harsh or hasty with those that are doubtful and wavering, but to give them Time and what Assistance we can for their better Information and Establishment." Third, "to represent to them faithfully and seriously the great Danger of denying the proper Godhead of *Christ* and of the *Holy Ghost*, and the malignant Influence it must have into the very Vitals of the Christian State and Worship." Fourth, that those who maintain such errors will not be recommended "to the Office of the Ministry by Ordination." Fifth, "if any already in the Ministry shall fall into that pernicious Error, and persist in it, and teach Men so, it will become our Duty, as we have Opportunity, to warn People of them."[23] Many of the ministers present at this meeting, which preceded the infamous meetings at Salters' Hall by approximately six months, were listed among the Subscribers in 1719.[24] At this point, however, they did not recommend subscription to those at Exeter.

The Committee of Thirteen at Exeter also appealed to London ministers on November 22, 1718.[25] The reply from London did not

---

[22] *A Plain and Faithful Narrative*, 9.

[23] *Plain and Faithful Narrative*, 11–12.

[24] It is worth noting that in these initial recommendations which were affirmed by twenty-five ministers, many of whom went on to be subscribers in the Salters' Hall controversy the next year, they did not recommend subscription to a confession of faith. If the "Mr. Hunt" who is a signatory, is in fact Jeremiah Hunt of Pinners' Hall, then he is the lone Nonsubscriber present at this meeting.

[25] Brockett, *Non-Conformity*, 89.

arrive until January 6, 1719, and included the names of Edmund Calamy, Jeremiah Smith, William Tong, Benjamin Robinson, and Thomas Reynolds.[26] The recommendation from London at that time was for neighboring ministers to be brought in to help advise.[27] They concluded that there are some theological errors so serious in nature that churches are justified in withdrawing from their ministers if they hold such views. Furthermore, they maintained that denying the consubstantial deity of Christ was in opposition to Scripture and the "common Faith of the reformed Churches." And finally, that it is the duty of ministers to oppose dangerous errors and "give reasonable satisfaction" of their own theological soundness.[28]

It was at this point that James Peirce appealed to his London friend and member of Parliament John Shute Barrington, a well-known defender of dissenting interests. A bill had been introduced in December 1718 by Lord Stanhope that, if passed, would repeal the Schism Act of 1714. Barrington was concerned that the Trinitarian controversy in Exeter might hinder the passage of the bill.[29] According to Roger Thomas, Barrington put together a set of advices in order to keep the peace in Exeter, and put them before "an unofficial committee of ministers and gentlemen on 5 February."[30] The advices then went before the Committee of the General Body of the Three Denominations, which approved the advices after debate and some changes. It was then decided by the

---

[26] Each of these men, Calamy excluded, were numbered among the Subscribers at the Salters' Hall.

[27] Brockett, *Non-Conformity*. These ministers were: John Ball of Honinton, William Horsham of Topsham, Samuel Hall and John Moore of Tiverton, John Walrond of Ottery, Josiah Eveleigh of Crediton, and Joseph Manston of Lympstone.

[28] *A Plain and Faithful Narrative*, 27-8.

[29] Roger Thomas notes: "Introduced to the House of Lords on 13 December, it received the Royal assent on 18 February, the day before the first meeting at Salters' Hall. See Roger Thomas, "The Non-Subscription Controversy amongst Dissenters in 1719: the Salters' Hall Debate," *The Journal of Ecclesiastical History* 4, no. 2 (1953): 168 n3.

[30] Thomas, "Non-Subscription," 170.

Committee to put the advices before the gathered body of London ministers of the Three Denominations. The intended goal, according to Calamy, was to add weight to the final decision.[31] This ultimately led to the infamous meetings at Salters' Hall.

The Salters' Hall Controversy

There are seven key dates for understanding the Salters' Hall controversy, each occurring between February and April of 1719. February 19 was the first official meeting at Salters' Hall when "the *Body* of *Protestant Dissenting Ministers* in, and about, *London*, were called together, to consider a Paper, containing *Advices for promoting Peace*, &c. Which Paper was recommended to them by their *Committee of Three Denominations*."[32] The ministers present on February 19 agreed to consider the advices paragraph by paragraph.

February 24 was the second meeting at Salters' Hall "at which Time the Names of all present were set down and then called over one by one; each *Denomination* being to approve or disapprove of such as were reputed to belong to them."[33] After the advices were debated for several hours it was agreed upon by a majority vote of fifty-seven to fifty-three "that *a Declaration concerning the Trinity should not be inserted in the Paper of Advices.*"[34] As Joseph Jekyl described the matter: "The Bible carried it by four."[35]

The third meeting at Salters' Hall, which resulted in the division of Subscribers and Nonsubscribers, occurred on March 3. The issue of inserting a declaration concerning the doctrine of the Trinity was revived at this meeting even though it had been at least

---

[31] Thomas, "Non-Subscription," 171.
[32] *An Authentick Account of Several Things Done and agreed upon by the Dissenting Ministers Lately assembled at Salters-Hall* (London, 1719), 18.
[33] *Authentick Account.*
[34] *Authentick Account*, 18–19.
[35] William Whiston, *Memoirs of the Life and Writings of William Whiston* (London, 1749), 220.

temporarily set aside in order to finish going through the advices. The group in favor of inserting the declaration, which would ultimately become known as the Subscribers, was not satisfied with the proceedings. Therefore, "Instead of this, they withdrew from our Assembly, and went *by* themselves, to subscribe their Names to a certain *Roll of Paper*, wherein was contain'd (as we were told) the *first Article* of the *Church of England*, and the 5th and 6th *Answers* in the *Assembly's Catechism*."[36] In a more colorful, but potentially apocryphal account, it is claimed that during this verbal scuffle someone shouted: "*You that are against Persecution, come up Stairs!* Which was pretty evenly balanced by one on the other side, calling out, *You that are for the Doctrine of the Trinity, stay below!*"[37] The Nonsubscribers continued to meet and consider the advices while the Subscribers apparently withdrew.[38] Following the March 3 meeting the two groups never met together again.

On March 9 the Subscribers met to finalize their advices, which were to be sent to Exeter. The Nonsubscribers met for the same purpose on the very next day, March 10. The Nonsubscribers' advices were sent to Exeter on March 17, but the Subscribers' advices were not sent until April 7. Both sets of advices arrived too

---

[36] *Authentick Account*, 19. The page is mistakenly numbered "16" in some copies of *An Authentick Account*.

[37] *An Account of the late Proceedings of the Dissenting Ministers at Salters-Hall. Occasioned By the Differences amongst their Brethren in the Country: With Some Thoughts concerning the Imposition of humane Forms for Articles of Faith. In a Letter to the Revd. Dr. Gale* (London, 1719), 10.

[38] According to *An Authentick Account*, the two groups remained together through the third point of their advices. Then we read: "Thus far we remained on *March* 3d. And then thought fit to adjourn further Consideration on these Advices till the following *Tuesday, March* 10th; ordering a Summons to be sent to every one of the Brethren who had withdrawn form us; which was accordingly done. We did particularly hope to have their Help in the IVth Article; and to have calmly debated, every Sentence and Word in it. Some Changes we our selves have made from what it was, both in *Substance* and *Form*; and, tho it looks to us, as it now stands, a very *Christian* and *reasonable Rule* of Conduct, yet we were not so set upon having our own Way, but we should have readily received any thing that had been clear and convincing, in order to have changed our Minds." See *Authentick Account*, 7-8.

late as a decision had already been made in Exeter. James Peirce and Joseph Hallet had been locked out of their churches on March 6.

The separate sets of advices and accompanying letters bear some resemblance, but also differ on key points. Both groups were in agreement that there were some doctrines so essential to the Christian faith that if rejected by a minister, the congregation was justified in withdrawing from that minister or the minister should withdraw from that congregation.[39] Such cases should be "managed *clearly*, *calmly*, and in the *Fear* of GOD, with Meekness and tender Compassion towards *all* with whom they are concerned."[40] Both groups affirmed that ministers should be directly addressed by those in their congregation, and then assemblies or neighboring ministers if necessary.[41]

The primary difference in the two sets of advices appeared near the end of each. The Nonsubscribers affirmed: "we think the Protestant Principle, that the *Bible is the only and the perfect Rule of Faith*," and that no one should "condemn any Man upon the Authority of Humane Decisions, or because he consents not to Humane Forms or Phrases." Instead, he is only "to be censured, as *not holding the Faith necessary to Salvation*, when it appears that he contradicts, or refuses to own, the *plain and express Declarations of Holy Scripture*, in what is there made necessary to be believed, and

---

[39] *An Authentick Account*, 5, 10; *A True Relation Of Some Proceedings At Salters-Hall By Those Ministers Who Sign'd The First Article of the Church of England, and The Answers to the Fifth and sixth Questions in the Assemblies Shorter Catechism. March 3. 1719.* (London, 1719), 11, 15.

[40] *True Relation*, 13.

[41] The two sets of advices differ slightly in emphases here, but seem to be similar in the main. *An Authentick Account* strongly emphasizes the necessity of certainty and multiple witnesses who are willing to testify against the minister privately if necessary. See *Authentick Account*, 7. *A True Relation*, instead of emphasizing the necessity of certainty and witnesses, although "care" and "caution" are recommended, moves more quickly to calling "for the Advice of Neighboring Ministers." See *True Relation*, 13. Again, they are similar in the main but differ in emphases.

in Matters there solely revealed."⁴² Yet this should not be interpreted as a total rejection of the value of human words and forms. The Nonsubscribers contended: "We further advise, that Catechisms and other Summaries of Christianity, and Expositions of Scripture by wise and learned, tho' fallible Men, should be regarded as great Helps to understand the Mind of God in the Scriptures."⁴³

Whereas both groups were clear that each congregation must determine what doctrines are worth dividing over, the Subscribers went further by stating:

> As we have with very good Reason declared the Right of the People to judge what those Doctrines are that will justify them in withdrawing from their Minister, so we take the Freedom to declare it as our Judgment, That *the Denying of the true and proper Divinity of the* Son *of* GOD *and the* HOLY SPIRIT, viz. *that they are One* GOD *with the* Father, *is an Error contrary to the* HOLY SCRIPTURES *and common Faith of the* REFORMED CHURCHES.⁴⁴

The Subscribers wanted those in Exeter to know that they affirmed the doctrine of the Trinity, and believed that, when rejected, it was an error worth separating over. They further declared their belief in the doctrine of the Trinity by including and subscribing to the first of the Thirty-Nine Articles. This was inserted at the beginning of *A True Relation*. They further noted that they had subscribed to the fifth and sixth answers of the Westminster Shorter Catechism.⁴⁵

We can conclude from this that the Subscribers and the Nonsubscribers at Salters' Hall shared some similarities in their

---

⁴² *Authentick Account*, 8–9.
⁴³ *Authentick Account*, 9.
⁴⁴ *True Relation*, 16.
⁴⁵ *True Relation*, 8, 17.

advices to Exeter. The Subscribers went to great lengths to demonstrate their own orthodoxy on the doctrine of the Trinity.[46] The Nonsubscribers, as will be noted in more detail below, were concerned to contend for their orthodoxy on the doctrine of the Trinity, but their advices focused primarily on the steps they thought fit for dealing with the disputes in Exeter. Yet the question of whether or not their lack of subscription necessarily served as a thinly veiled disguise for heterodoxy remains unanswered.

Early Accounts of Salters' Hall

When William Tong called together twenty-five ministers to meet informally at Salters' Hall on August 25, 1718 to respond to John Walrond's letter concerning Exeter, they stated rather clearly in their response that they were not aware of any great progress of Arianism among their ministers in the greater London area: "We cannot say that we have no Apprehension of the breaking forth of the liker Errors here, but we know of none among us, hitherto that have *openly* avowed them, and of but very *Few* that own themselves

---

[46] The disagreement about what needed to be accomplished at Salters' Hall is apparent in a work entitled *Plain Dealing*. I have found no work with stronger rebukes and accusations than this work. One quote will demonstrate that the author understands the issue at hand to be the doctrine of the Trinity: "It began first among those of the Church of *England*, since which, some of the *Dissenting Ministers* have been poyson'd therewith, which causes no small Pain and Grief of the Heart to those who are *Orthodox* in the Faith. This making such a Noise in the World, it was at length thought necessary that the Dissenting Ministers of *London*, under the three Denominations, should meet at *Salter's-Hall*, there to consult Measures, how to remove that Scandal that was thrown upon 'em by the Enemies of the *Christian Religion*, where accordingly it was propos'd that a *Declaration* should be publickly subscrib'd by all those Gentlemen in the Ministry, in Order to convince the World, that they did believe the Doctrine of the *Trinity*, oin the same Sense that all the Protestant Churches in the World do. This was accordingly done by several, whose Hearts were right with God, and yet there were many at the same Time, who would by no Means be prevail'd upon, or give their Consent to subscribe their Names thereto, to the great Triumph of the *Arians* and *Socinians*." See *Plain Dealing: Or A Friendly Reproof to the Reverend Mr. Willian Bush and Mr. David Jennings, Both Dissenting Ministers near Wapping; for Refusing to Subscribe the Declaration for the Ever Blessed Trinity* (London, 1719), 4-5.

to be in Doubt and Suspence about them."⁴⁷ Just six months prior to the controversy at Salters' Hall, some of the leading Presbyterian ministers in and around London could confidently declare that there was no great outbreak of Arianism among their ministers.

To return to the central issue at hand, the debate following Salters' Hall centered on what the source of the disagreement between the Subscribers and Nonsubscribers really was. Were the Nonsubscribers merely opposed to requiring subscription to extrabiblical words and phrases and orthodox in their understanding of the Trinity? Or, was their opposition to subscription merely a disguise for their heterodox views on the Trinity? Subscribers and onlookers alike questioned the orthodoxy of some of the Nonsubscribers from the outset. But the Nonsubscribers openly declared their orthodoxy. They contended that they were opposed to forced subscription rather than a historic, Christian theology of the Trinity.

The Nonsubscribers' Account

The Nonsubscribers at Salters' Hall were insistent that they were not opposed to the doctrine of the Trinity. In their letter to Exeter dated March 17, 1719 they wrote:

> We add our earnest Supplications that God would accompany them [the advices] with his Blessing to establish Peace and Truth amongst us: And freely declare, that we utterly disown the *Arian* doctrine, and sincerely believe the Doctrine of the Blessed Trinity, and the proper Divinity of our Lord Jesus Christ, which we apprehend to be clearly revealed in the Holy Scriptures; But are far from condemning any who appear to be with us in the Main, tho' they should chuse not to declare themselves in other than Scripture-Terms or not in Ours.⁴⁸

---

[47] *Plain and Faithful Narrative*, 11.
[48] *Authentick Account*, 15–16.

Jesse F. Owens

Some took issue with this language, desiring even greater clarity on the doctrine of the Trinity, which could be found in the Westminster Shorter Catechism or the Thirty-Nine Articles.[49] As one critic insightfully noted, the Nonsubscribers were willing to use extrabiblical words and phrases in this declaration.[50]

Edmund Calamy
Even the respected Presbyterian pastor Edmund Calamy (1671–1732), who refused to be involved in the controversy by joining either party, contended that the issue at Salters' Hall was subscription and not the doctrine of the Trinity. A Mr. Chalmers urged Calamy the day before the March 3 meeting to be present in order that he might help defend the cause of orthodoxy. Yet Calamy was resolute that the issue at stake was not the doctrine of the Trinity. "I told him," Calamy wrote, "as for the true eternal divinity of the Lord Jesus Christ, I was very ready to declare for it, at that time or any other, and durst not in conscience be at all backward to it." He continued, "But I could upon good grounds assure him, that was not the point in question among those that were to meet together on the day following."[51] Chalmers, who apparently had been present at the meeting, upon his return visit with Calamy, "was convinced most fully that I [Calamy] was in the right, and he

---

[49] *Plain Dealing*, 11-12. Edward Wallin, a Particular Baptist Subscriber at Salters' Hall, in a letter to Elisha Callender, a Baptist pastor in Boston Massachusetts, uses the very same words "proper divinity" by which he seems to mean that the Son is consubstantial with the Father. See, Isaac Backus, *A History of New England Baptists With Particular Reference to the Denomination of Christians Called Baptists*, Second Edition (Newton, MA: The Backus Historical Society, 1871), 1:491.

[50] *Plain Dealing*, 11.

[51] Edmund Calamy, *An Historical Account of My Own Life, With Some Reflections on the Time I Have Lived In*, Second Edition (London: Henry Colburn and Richard Bentley, New Burlington Street, 1830), 2:414–415.

[Chalmers] was in the wrong."⁵² According to Calamy, the point in question at Salters' Hall was not the doctrine of the Trinity.

Edward Wallin

Edward Wallin (1678–1733), a well-respected Particular Baptist minister, was numbered among the Subscribers at Salters' Hall. By all accounts, including that of the renowned John Gill, Wallin was a thoroughly orthodox, godly minister.⁵³ Gill preached Wallin's funeral sermon and said of him: "Besides a large experience of the grace of God, and a considerable share of light and knowledge in the great truths of the Gospel; he had an heavenly skill to lay open the wretchedness and miserable state and condition of sinners by nature, and to set forth the glory of Christ in his person, blood, righteousness, and sacrifice."⁵⁴ Edward Wallin accepted the call to pastor the Maze Pond congregation in London at the age of twenty-seven, which he pastored until his death twenty-seven years later. Edward Wallin's son, Benjamin, followed him as pastor at Maze Pond with their pastoral tenures there covering nearly three-quarters of the eighteenth century.⁵⁵

Wallin recounted the Exeter and Salters' Hall controversies in 1720 in a letter to Elisha Callendar, a Baptist Minister in Boston, Massachusetts. In the letter Wallin provided a balanced interpretation of Salters' Hall, noting that there may have been some anti-Trinitarians present, but that the majority were orthodox, and concerned primarily with maintaining Christian liberty. After recounting the insistence of one party to subscribe a declaration of

---

⁵² Calamy, *Historical Account*, 2:416.
⁵³ John Gill, *Job's Creed: or, Confession of Faith. A Sermon Occasioned by the Death of the Reverend Mr. Edward Wallin, who Departed this Life June 12, 1733 in the 55th Year of his Age. Preached June 18.* (London, 1733).
⁵⁴ Gill, *Job's Creed*, 42–3.
⁵⁵ Terry Wolever, "Edward Wallin 1678-1733 Benjamin Wallin 1711-1782" in *The British Particular Baptists*, eds. Michael A. G. Haykin and Terry Wolever (Springfield, MO: Particular Baptist Press, 2018), 4:45.

their faith in the Trinity, and the other party's desire to continue considering the advices paragraph by paragraph, Wallin addressed the issue at hand. His account is worth quoting at length:

> Some of the too warm among the non-subscribers would fain fix the odious charge of persecution on the other, while they again, with full as much warmth, would fix the charge of Arianism upon them. But this severity is not allowed by the greatest part of either side of the question; and I hope time will produce a better temper in both parties...As I am satisfied that some among the non-subscribers are gone too far into some of the distinctive notions of Arius, so I think some of the subscribers have given too much ground to jealousy, they intended to set up those forms as a test of orthodoxy, and the signing of them as necessary to persons being useful in the ministry. But I dare say for the much greater part of both sides, that they intended no evil to their differing brethren; and that it was a zeal for the doctrine of the Trinity, and the real divinity of our Saviour, which made some subscribe the articles, and not any desire to impose upon others; and that those who refused the subscription, did it with a design to maintain Christian liberty, rather than any design to encourage or promote Arianism. There is no great difference in the number of either side; but I think there are not so many of our denomination among the non-subscribers as are on the other side; and though I cannot say that there are none of our ministers who too much favor the new scheme, yet I may venture to say in general, that our ministers, especially those of the Particular [Baptist] denomination, are sound in the faith, as to the real divinity of Christ, and the true doctrine of the Blessed Trinity. Therefore those who upbraid you with their being contrary, act either from prejudice or misinformation. But such have been the visible consequences of this difference, that brotherly

love and charity, that indispensable ornament of the Christian religion, have been greatly lost in these debates.[56]

Wallin's firsthand account provides several helpful insights. First, as Calamy noted, tempers and suspicion abounded during and after the meetings at Salters' Hall. Second, there were some anti-Trinitarians present at Salters' Hall. Third, the majority of the ministers at Salters' Hall were not anti-Trinitarians. Fourth, the disagreement at hand was primarily about what was most necessary at that time—subscription as a means of demonstrating one's personal orthodoxy, or, continuing with the examination of the advices to be sent to Exeter. Therefore, according to Calamy and Wallin, Salter's Hall should not be understood primarily as an acceptance or rejection of the doctrine of the Trinity.

An Orthodox, Nonsubscribing Tradition

In a letter to Samuel Mather dated July 28, 1731, John Walrond claimed, more than a decade after the Salters' Hall Controversy, that there were "three sorts" of Dissenters: "those who have fallen into Arian or Arminian errors;" those that are "very sound;" "and a middle sort, the most numerous, that profess the same faith, but are so indifferent about it, and indulgent to the erroneous, that they seem to be with us in principle, but with them in interest, loving them better with their errors, than others with the truth as it is in Jesus."[57] It was Walrond who had been one of James Peirce's fiercest foes at Exeter. But Walrond's point is instructive for a balanced interpretation of Salters' Hall. For at Salters' Hall there seems to have been a largely orthodox, nonsubscribing party, which, for the General Baptists and Presbyterians in particular, finds its historical and theological roots in Thomas Grantham and Richard Baxter respectively.

---

[56] Backus, *History of New England Baptists*, 492–493.
[57] *The Christian Examiner* 5 no. 5 (September-October: 1828), 369.

Jesse F. Owens

Thomas Grantham

Thomas Grantham (1633–1692) was one of the foremost English General Baptist theologians of the seventeenth century. Grantham was thoroughly orthodox in his understanding of the doctrine of the Trinity. In his *magnum opus, Christianismus Primitivus* (1678), Grantham even reprints the Nicene Creed. Elsewhere in *Christianismus Primitivus* Grantham wrote: "But that the Son (I speak now in respect of his Divine Essence only) and the Holy Spirit are Eternal, as the Father is Eternal, or consequently of the same Nature or Essence, may be gathered from these Testimonies."[58] Grantham went on to quote a variety of texts that demonstrated that the Son was consubstantial with the Father regarding his deity.

Yet Grantham was hesitant to require others to use extrabiblical words and phrases. According to Grantham, the word "Trinity" was in "no way offensive to Christianity." Yet he concluded: "It is not necessary to impose words upon any Man which God himself hath not used, by which to make known himself. Yet truly this term, *The Trinity*, hath a very near affinity with the Language of the Holy Ghost."[59] This hesitancy led Grantham scholar, Clint Bass, to reasonably conclude: "Had Grantham been at the Salters' Hall meeting in 1719, he might have been a Non-subscriber."[60] There is, in fact, a direct connection to Grantham at Salters' Hall. Nathaniel Foxwell who early in his ministry was sent by the General Assembly to assist Grantham, "in the Ministerial work of the Gospell" at Norwich, was a Nonsubscriber at Salters' Hall.[61] Foxwell left Norwich in 1699, and served at Hart-street as an assistant for one year before moving to Paul's Alley, Barbican. The

---

[58] Thomas Grantham, *Christianismus Primitivus: Or, The Ancient Christian Religion* (London, 1678), Book II, Part I, 40.

[59] Grantham, *Christianismus Primitivus*.

[60] Clint C. Bass, *Thomas Grantham (1633-1692) and General Baptist Theology* (Oxford: Regent's Park College Press, 2013), 189.

[61] Whitley, *Minutes of the General Assembly*, 31.

larger point surrounding Grantham, however, is that he potentially serves as an example of an orthodox, nonsubscribing tradition among the English General Baptists.[62]

Richard Baxter
Richard Baxter had an unmistakable influence at Exeter and Salters' Hall as his writings were regularly referred to, and the influence of his thought seems quite apparent. Baxter's influence on Salters' Hall is particularly apparent in *A Letter to Mr. Robinson* (1719). The author wrote concerning an "imposing Spirit": "Mr. *Baxter* ... gives us an Instance of this High Church Temper in his Time, that bears a very near Resemblance to the Creed-making Disposition that prevails at this Day among us."[63] Baxter referred to himself as a "meer Christian." Paul C. H. Lim notes that the title was first employed by the English Socinian, John Biddle, not Baxter.[64] Baxter used the term to denote a sort of strict biblicism that emphasized the supremacy of Scripture over all confessions, creeds, and councils. While many English Protestants might have

---

[62] The English General Baptist, Joseph Hooke, carried Grantham's legacy on subscription into the eighteenth century. Hooke was an ardent defender of orthodoxy, demonstrated by his work *The Socinian Slain With The Sword of the Spirit* (1700), which was a reply to Daniel Allen's *The Moderate Trinitarian* (1699). In 1729, ten years after the Salters' Hall controversy, Hooke published a work entitled *Creed-Making and Creed-Imposing Considered; And The Divinity of Christ, And The Doctrine of the Trinity Defended* (London, 1729). In it, Hooke was strongly in favor of the composition of creeds and confessions of faith. Hooke wrote: "God *makes* the Creed; and Man declares it, according to the best of his Understanding; and calls it a *Creed*, a Thing to be believed." Furthermore, Hooke was in favor of separating from and even expelling pastors who rejected essential biblical doctrines such as the Trinity. He was resolutely opposed to any unity or fellowship that was not "founded in our faith." But Hooke followed Grantham on subscription: "This is my Judgment, concerning imposing of *Creeds*, or *Confessions of Faith of human Composure*; and I have, upon divers Occasions, declared my self to be against imposing *such Creeds*; wherein I agree with the *blessed* Mr. Grantham, and many others, both antient and modern Writers of good Esteem in the Church." See *Creed-Making and Creed-Imposing*, 3, 7, 10.

[63] *A Letter to Mr. Robinson* (London, 1719), 13.

[64] Paul C. H. Lim, *Mystery Unveiled: The Crisis of the Trinity in Early Modern England* (Oxford: Oxford University Press, 2012), 240.

shared Baxter's views in principle, Baxter went beyond merely affirming the supremacy of Scripture to regularly critiquing the bishops involved in the councils at Nicaea and Ephesus. The intended purpose of Baxter's attacks on early church councils was to demonstrate not only that councils may err, but to expose the immoral qualities of "thuggish" bishops such as Cyril of Alexandria.[65] As Lim explains, "Baxter saw sanctification or 'laborious holiness' as an existential proof of the theological pudding. Seeing the utter absence of such saintly dispositions and behaviors at Nicaea and Ephesus was what turned Baxter off from being enthusiastic about the doctrines formulated therein."[66] Baxter provocatively asked, *"Did the Primitive Church require Subscription to all our 39 Articles, or to any more than the words of Scripture?"*[67] The cumulative effect of Baxter's critiques, however, was that his own orthodoxy was called into question.[68]

Baxter's consistent concern was ecclesiastical unity rather than theological uniformity.[69] He maintained his hope for some sort of ecclesiastical unity, even after the Glorious Revolution and the Toleration Act of 1689.[70] Baxter's desire for unity often led him to oppose the stringent theological precisian of theologians such as John Owen and Francis Cheynell, which Baxter believed bred unnecessary division. Related to Baxter's desire for unity was his opposition to creedal subscription. Baxter boldy asserted in 1654: "No particular Words in the World are *Essentials* of our

---

[65] Lim, *Mystery Unveiled*, 255.

[66] Lim, *Mystery Unveiled*, 248.

[67] Richard Baxter in Lim, *Mystery Unveiled*, 247.

[68] Lim, *Mystery Unveiled*, 247.

[69] Paul Chang-Ha Lim, *In Pursuit of Purity: Richard Baxter's Puritan Ecclesiology in Its Seventeenth-Century Context* (Leiden; Boston: Brill, 2004).

[70] N. H. Keeble, "'Take heed of being too forward in imposing on others: orthodoxy and heresy in the Baxterian tradition," in *Heresy, Literature, and Politics in Early Modern English Culture*, eds. David Lowenstein and John Marshall (Cambridge: Cambridge University Press, 2006), 297.

In Essence One, in Persons Three

Religion."[71] Keeble notes regarding this statement, "What lay behind these words was a deep-seated suspicion of credal formulae, confessions, and platforms."[72] Baxter exhibited a strong primitivist impulse, which he believed, required a return to the doctrinal simplicity of the early church. Baxter concluded: "The great cause of our uncharitable censures and divisions, hath been departing from the Antient simplicity of Faith, and also from the sufficiency of the holy Scriptures, to be the Rule and Test of Faith."[73] For Baxter, the essentials of the Christian faith could be summarized in the Apostles' Creed, the Lord's Prayer, and the Ten Commandments.[74] These, he believed, were sufficient tests of orthodoxy. When it was objected that Papists and Socinians could subscribe these statements, Baxter shockingly replied: "So much the better, and so much the fitter it is to be the Matter of our Concord."[75] Yet as Lim rightly points out, one would be remiss to overlook the rest of what Baxter said:

> if you are afraid of Communion with *Papists* and *Socinians*, it must not be avoided by making a new Rule or Test of Faith which they will not Subscribe to, or by forcing others to Subscribe to more than *they* can do, but by calling them to account whenever in Preaching or Writing they contradict or abuse the Truth to which they have Subscribed. This is the Work of the *Government*.[76]

Such was Baxter's view of subscription and his desire for unity. He certainly was not a proto-Unitarian in his desire for unity and his opposition to subscription. But Baxter did not believe the multiplication of creeds and confessions or the requirement of

---

[71] Richard Baxter in Keeble, "'Take heed of being too forward,'" 282.
[72] Keeble, "'Take heed of being too forward,'" 282.
[73] Richard Baxter in Keeble, "'Take heed of being too forward,'" 282.
[74] Keeble, "'Take heed of being too forward,'" 284.
[75] Baxter in Keeble, "'Take heed of being too forward,'" 284.
[76] Baxter in Lim, *In Pursuit of Purity*, 163.

Jesse F. Owens

subscription to extrabiblical words and phrases to be the answer to stamping out theological heterodoxy. As Calamy, who collated and printed Baxter's works, carried Baxter into the eighteenth century, the Baxterian tradition, particularly as it relates to a sort of credal minimalism and opposition to the requirement of subscription, was significant at Salters' Hall.[77]

Conclusion

The case for the majority of the Nonsubscribers at Salters' Hall being theologically orthodox regarding the doctrine of the Trinity, but opposed to the requirement of subscription to extrabiblical words and phrases, is strong. There certainly were some anti-Trinitarians at Salters' Hall.[78] The decades following Salters' Hall saw an increase of anti-Trinitarianism throughout England, particularly in the Church of England, among the Presbyterians, and among the General Baptists. Yet the proliferation of anti-Trinitarianism in the decades following Salters' Hall does not necessarily entail a wholesale theological deviation from the doctrine of the Trinity among the Nonsubscribers. The history of eighteenth-century English Dissent proves that this latitudinarian spirit, which pervaded Salters' Hall, did open the door even wider for theological deviation. The *sola Scriptura* principle, which was in many cases more akin to *nuda Scriptura*, could not stem the rising

---

[77] The influence of Baxter does in fact seem to loom large at Salters' Hall in particular. Baxter is cited in some of the pamphlets that came out of the Salters' Hall controversy, which certainly demonstrates a connection between the opposition to subscription at Salters' Hall, and Baxter's opposition to subscription. Baxter had been dead for less than thirty years when the controversy occurred. Therefore, while it would be a mistake to see Baxter as some sort of proto-Unitarian, as his opposition heterodoxy was clear, it would also be an overreaction to such claims to see Baxter's approach to subscription as having no influence at Salters' Hall. This point is further bolstered by the connection that Keeble makes between Baxter and Calamy. See *A Letter to Mr. Robinson* (London, 1719), 13.

[78] Benjamin Avery (Presbyterian) and Nathaniel Lardner (Independent) are the most likely anti-Trinitarians at Salters' Hall. That is not to say that others may not be added to the list through further examination.

tide of heterodoxy. No matter how well-intended the Nonsubscribers at Salters' Hall were, if they hoped to maintain any sort of theological orthodoxy on the doctrine of the Trinity, their categorical opposition to subscription proved unwise.

4
John Gill (1697–1771) and the Eternal Begotten Word of God

Jonathan E. Swan

The Baptist pastor John Gill (1697–1771) believed the doctrine of eternal generation was vital to the Christian faith. While he firmly held to the doctrine of eternal generation, counting it as indispensable for grounding distinctions between the persons within the Godhead, he denied that the divine essence is communicated in generation. Generation, for Gill, entailed only the begetting of persons, and spoke to the ordering and personal relations between the Trinitarian Persons. As the second Person, the Son is from the Father, but as God, he is of himself. This understanding of eternal generation flowed from Gill's commitment to the aseity of all the divine Persons. According to Gill, each of the divine Persons fully possesses the essence without any communication of essence and without respect to their ordered subsistence. Each person equally, fully, and eternally partakes of the divine essence of himself. Gill's affirmation of eternal generation was strengthened and elaborated by his understanding of the Son as the divine Word. Gill's understanding of the Son as the divine Word incorporated the analogy of the mind, which was further understood by other Scriptural images and was further apprehended by the Son's identification as Wisdom. Gill understood these analogies and names as mutually defining for understanding the nature of the Son of God. The central theological implications of this divine name, namely, the Son's deity, eternality, and distinct personality, were all based on Gill's reading of Scripture, most notably in the Gospel of John.[1]

---

[1] Although it cannot be drawn out in this essay, when Gill denied a communication of essence as part of eternal generation, he was following a trajectory set by Calvin's doctrine of the Son as *autotheos*. The significance of this is found in the fact that Calvin's understanding of eternal generation, as it pertained to the nature of the Son as *autotheos*, ran counter to the doctrine as it had been developed and understood by many throughout church history, what Brannon Ellis calls "classical Trinitarianism." It was also the minority view among the reformed, even after Calvin. Yet, Gill followed the trajectory set by Calvin in his understanding of eternal generation and its relation to aseity. The above arguments regarding Calvin, classical Trinitarianism, and the reformed response can be found in Brannon Ellis' work, which ignited my investigation into the same issues in Gill's theology. Brannon Ellis, *Calvin, Classical Trinitarianism, and the Aseity of the Son* (Oxford: Oxford University Press, 2012). I am thankful for Jacob Denhollander who pointed this book out to me. Conversations with Jacob and Dr. Tyler Wittman were important in helping me piece together these ideas for the original paper (unpublished, "The Fountain of Life: Eternal Generation and the Aseity of the Son in the Theology of John Gill (1697-1771)") from which this section of my essay comes, which is part of a larger project related to Gill's theology and its relation to the development of Trinitarian theology. For discussions of Calvin's view in relation to the reformed theologians that followed him, see Ellis, *Calvin, Classical Trinitarianism, and the Aseity of the Son*, 152-170. According to Mark Jones, Calvin's doctrine of aseity was a point of contention at the Westminster Assembly. His main point is that Calvin's doctrine of aseity—that eternal generation is a generation of person apart from a communication of essence, was the minority view at the Assembly. Jones demonstrates, however, that Calvin did have some supporters, some of whom understood Calvin's statements differently. Jones shows that there were some who took Calvin's view to at least allow for a communication of essence in generation, although wrongly. Quoting Chad Van Dixhorn's Ph.D. thesis on the Assembly, Jones notes that those called "Autotheanites" were not satisfied with any of the measures used to bring together Calvin and the Nicene Creed. Mark Jones, "John Calvin's Reception at the Westminster Assembly (1643-1649)," *Church History and Religious Culture* 91, no. 1-2 (2011): 115-122. Beeke and Jones note the differences among the Reformed regarding the exact meaning of eternal generation: "The doctrine of eternal generation of the Son was agreed upon by all Reformed theologians. What they did not all agree upon, however, was the precise meaning of the Father's generation of the Son. So it was possible to be Nicean and yet have somewhat differing views on what it means for the Son to be "God of God." Consequently, the Reformed orthodox all held to the aseity (self-existence) of God the Son, but with different nuances." They do, however, make the point to say that Calvin's position was the minority view among the Puritans. They show that while most of the Reformed orthodox affirmed the aseity of the Son, they did so while also affirming that the Son's essence is communicated as part of generation. Joel R. Beeke and Mark Jones, *A Puritan Theology: Doctrine for Life* (Grand Rapids, MI: Reformation Heritage Books, 2012), 95-97. Furthermore, Muller notes that "The radical statement of the Son's aseity found in Calvin's trinitarian polemic is not echoed by all of the early orthodox Reformed theologians." Muller highlights the diversity among the early Reformed orthodox and outlines the importance of *aseity* during the

Jonathan E. Swan

Eternal Generation

With respect to distinguishing the Persons of the Trinity, the doctrine of eternal generation was an absolute necessity for Gill.[2] Without it, none of the personal distinctions hold among the members of the Trinity. It is fundamental to the Christian religion. Gill referred to it as "the distinguishing criterion of the christian religion, and what gives it preference to all others, and upon which all the important doctrines of it depend; even upon the Sonship of Christ as a divine person; and as by generation, even eternal

---

eras of high and late orthodoxy in the face of Arminian and anti-Trinitarian rejections of the Son's *aseity*. Importantly, by highlighting Thomas Ridgley, Muller pointed out that "In the era of late orthodoxy, particularly among the English writings, extended controversy over Socinianism and Arianism yielded further worries over the suitability of trinitarian terminology ... arguments concerning the communication of essence from the Father to the Son, could be viewed as at best unwarranted and in the worst case fundamentally destructive of the doctrine of the Trinity." Richard A. Muller, *Post-Reformation Reformed Dogmatics: The Rise and Development of Reformed Orthodoxy, ca. 1520 to ca 1725: Volume Four: The Triunity of God*, Second Edition, vol. 4 (Grand Rapids, MI: Baker Academic, 2006), 4:326-332. The most thorough examination of Gill's Trinitarianism is still Steven Godett's unpublished dissertation. Steven Tshombe Godet, "The Trinitarian Theology of John Gill (1697-1771): Context, Sources, and Controversy" (Ph.D. Dissertation, The Southern Baptist Theological Seminary, 2015). See also Park's chapters on the doctrine of God and the Trinity: Hong-Gyu Park, "Grace and Nature in the Theology of John Gill (1697-1771)" (Ph.D. Dissertation, University of Aberdeen, 2001), 151-256.

[2] Not only did Gill write his *The Doctrine of the Trinity* (1731/1752)—a theological treatise on the Trinity—in order to protect the church he pastored, he also wrote a work defending eternal generation from an historical perspective. In that work, titled *A Dissertation Concerning the Eternal Sonship of Christ* (1768), Gill attempted to demonstrate the importance of eternal generation, arguing that all "sound and orthodox" theologians have held to eternal generation: "Now since it appears that all the sound and orthodox writes have unanimously declared for the eternal generation and Sonship of Christ in all ages, and that those only of an unsound mind and judgment, and corrupt in other things as well as this, and many of them men impure lives and vile principles, have declared against it, such must be guilty of great temerity and rashness to join in an opposition with the one against the other; and to oppose a doctrine the church of God has always held, and especially being what the scriptures abundantly bear testimony unto, and is a matter of such moment and importance, being a fundamental doctrine of the Christian religions, from those of Pagans, Jews and Mahometans, who all believe in God, and generally in one God, but none of them believe in the Son of God: that is peculiar to the christian religion." John Gill, "A Dissertation Concerning the Eternal Sonship of Christ," in *Sermons and Tracts*, 1814 ed.; repr. (Choteau, MT: Old Paths Gospel Press, 1999), 6:221.

generation. Without this the doctrine of the Trinity can never be supported."[3] The generation of the Son not only distinguishes the Son and the Father, but it also reveals the distinction between the Spirit and the Father and Son:

> If one of these distinct Persons is a Father, in the divine nature, and another a Son in the divine nature, there must be something in the divine nature which is the ground of the relation, and distinguishes the one from the other; and can be nothing else than generation, and which distinguishes the third Person from them both, as neither begetting nor begotten. From generation arises the relation, and from relation distinct personality ... Upon the whole, it is easy to observe that the distinction of Persons in the Deity depends on the generation of the Son; take away that, which would destroy the relation between the first and second Persons, and the distinction drops.[4]

This relation within the Godhead between the divine Persons is tied to the very nature of God and is thus eternal. Since "no moment and instant can be given or pointed at, neither in eternity nor in time, in which Christ was not the begotten Son of the Father," he must be eternally begotten. Thus, Gill stated, there is warrant for calling it "eternal generation."[5] Rather than thinking of eternal generation as priority of time between the Father and Son, Gill considered it prudent, when speaking of divine generation, to think of priority of ordering. Thus, for Gill, eternal generation not only speaks to personal distinctions within the Godhead, but also of *taxis*.[6]

---

[3] John Gill, *A Complete Body of Doctrinal and Practical Divinity: Or A System of Evangelical Truths, Deduced from the Sacred Scriptures*, 1839 ed.; repr. (Paris, AR: The Baptist Standard Bearer, 1989), 144.
[4] Gill, *Body of Doctrinal and Practical Divinity*, 142.
[5] Gill, *Body of Doctrinal and Practical Divinity*, 145.
[6] Gill, *Body of Doctrinal and Practical Divinity*, 145.

As Gill understood it, eternal generation is the begetting of person, not essence. This is abundantly clear in not only his doctrinal statements, but in his voluminous commentary on Scripture. According to Gill, "as in natural, so in divine generation, person begets person, and not essence begets essence." And as it is a begetting of a person, it is done in the divine essence. Thus, Gill asserted, "and this begetting is not *out* of, but *in* the divine essence; it being an immanent and internal act of God." Eternal generation, for Gill, is an eternal act of God's life in himself. It distinguishes the persons in the Godhead and from it arise the distinct personalities of the Father and Son that are mutually dependent on one another. Upon consideration of it, one must remove any impure and imperfect notions which allow for "division and multiplication, priority and posteriority, dependence, and the like." But the mode or manner of generation cannot be known, "we must be content to be ignorant of it."[7] Gill's exposition of Psalm 2:7 evinces his consistency on these points:

> He is the true, proper, natural, and eternal Son of God, and as such declared, owned, and acknowledged by Jehovah the Father, as in these words; the foundation of which relation lies in what follows: *this day have I begotten thee*; which act of begetting refers not to the nature, nor to the office, but the person of Christ; not to his nature, not to his divine nature, which is common with the Father and Spirit; wherefore if his was begotten, theirs must be also ... but it has respect to his person; for, as in human generation, person begets person, and like begets like, so in divine generation; but care must be taken to remove all imperfection from it, such as divisibility and multiplication of essence, priority and posteriority, dependence, and the like: nor can the modus or manner of it be conceived or explained by us."[8]

---

[7] Gill, *Body of Doctrinal and Practical Divinity*, 157-158.

[8] John Gill, *Exposition of the Old and New Testaments*, 1809-1810 ed.; repr. ed. (Paris, Arkansas: The Baptist Standard Bearer, 2006), 3:531, emphasis original.

The Aseity of the Son

Gill's comments regarding the nature of God reveal his understanding of aseity belonging to each person in the Godhead. In his *Body of Doctrinal Divinity*, Gill set out three basic guidelines for understanding God's nature. First, all concepts of God as corporeal must be thrown aside. Second, "The description of God, as a Spirit, teaches us to ascribe to God all the excellencies to be found in spirits in a more eminent manner, and to consider them as transcendent and infinite in him." Third, God is a "simple and uncompounded Being, and does not consist in parts."[9]

As Gill conceived it, God's spiritual and simple essence must be ascribed to all three Persons of the Godhead. Additionally, each Person must be understood to possess the essence of himself, without respect to imminent procession. Gill was emphatic on this point, and in his chapter in the *Body of Doctrinal Divinity* regarding the nature of God, he makes this clear. Of the way in which each person partakes of the essence, Gill stated,

> This nature is common to the three persons in God, but not communicated from one to another; they each of them partake of it, and possess it as one undivided nature; they all enjoy it; it is not part of it that is enjoyed by one, and a part of it by another, but the whole by each; as "all the fullness of the Godhead dwells in Christ," so in the holy Spirit; and of the Father, there will be no doubt; these equally subsists in the unity of the divine essence, and that without any derivation or communication of it from one to another.[10]

Much of what Gill asserted in this statement was affirmed by all Trinitarians. All affirmed that each Person fully possesses the fullness of the divine essence. All affirmed that Father, Son, and Spirit each subsists in full equality in the divine essence. But not all were

---

[9] Gill, *Body of Doctrinal and Practical Divinity*, 31–34.
[10] Gill, *Body of Doctrinal and Practical Divinity*, 30.

agreed as to the manner in which the essence is possessed.[11] Gill twice in this short excerpt denies a communication of essence between the divine persons. For him, the essence is shared in such a way that communication or derivation is unnecessary. Each fully partake of the essence of himself.

Gill, knowing the classical understanding of eternal generation, acknowledged that orthodox Trinitarians disagreed on this point: "I know it is represented by some, who, otherwise are sound in the doctrine of the Trinity, that the divine nature is communicated from the Father to the Son and Spirit, and that he is *fons Deitatis*, 'the fountain of Deity.'" Nevertheless, he considered this way of speaking to be theologically problematic, arguing that these are "unsafe phrases; since they seem to imply a priority in the Father to the other two persons; for he that communicates must, at least in order of nature, and according to our conception of things, be prior to whom the communication is made; and that he has a superabundant plenitude of Deity in him, previous to this communication." For Gill, a communication of the essence is problematic because it seems to suggest a priority of the Father. At the very least, it implies a priority in ordering, but it also may suggest temporal ordering. It additionally may suggest that one of the persons possesses the Deity in a greater measure than the others. For these reasons, Gill thought it best to consider the divine sharing of essence in the following way: "It is better to say, that they are self-existent, and exist together in the same undivided essence; and jointly, equally, and as early one as the other, possess the same nature." Thus, there is not one person who, in the personal ordering of the Trinity, communicates the essence to the others. There are simply three, who relate personally to one

---

[11] This is the historical issue that Ellis addresses in his work, positing continuity and development with Calvin on the issue regarding communication of essence as part of eternal generation. See his introduction: Ellis, *Calvin and the Aseity of the Son*, 1-15. See also the citations and discussion in footnote 1 on the Reformed tradition.

another in the essence, with each person possessing the essence of himself.[12]

In his earlier treatise, *The Doctrine of the Trinity* (1731/1752), Gill affirmed the same idea in his discussion about the personality of the Father:

> Now when we call the Father the first person in the Trinity, we do not suppose that he is the first, in order of nature, time, or causality; as if the Father was *fons Deitatis*, the fountain of the Deity; expressions which some good men have made use of with no ill design: But since an ill use has been made of them, by artful and designing men, 'tis time for us to lay them aside. As the Father is God of himself, so the Son is God of himself, and the Spirit is God of himself. They all three exist together, and necessarily exist, and subsist distinctly by themselves in one undivided nature. The one is not before the other, nor more excellent than the other.[13]

The rule, for Gill, is that each Person fully possesses the divine essence, in all of its perfection—of himself—and this in the same manner. *Taxis*, and mode of subsistence, does not factor into this possession in any way. The personal relations are not considered with respect to how each Person partakes of the essence. Each Person, particularly considered as God, is God of himself. For Gill, neither the Son nor the Spirit have the divine nature bestowed upon them through any form of communicative action within the Godhead, regardless of how it is defined. As each person is God, so each person is God of himself.[14]

---

[12] Gill, *Body of Doctrinal and Practical Divinity*, 30–31.

[13] John Gill, *The Doctrine of the Trinity, Stated and Vindicated. Being the Substance of Several Discourses on that Important Subject; Reduc'd into the Form of a Treatise*, 2nd Edition (London: George Keith, 1752), 83–84. The first edition of this work was printed in 1731. All citations in this essay refer to the second edition of 1752.

[14] Gill's comments regarding the specific language of aseity were certainly reactionary. They provide a helpful glance into the reality of anti-Trinitarianism during his

Jonathan E. Swan

The Eternally Begotten Word of God

While Gill did not conceive of eternal generation as involving a communication of essence from the Father to the Son, he found help in Scripture for understanding the nature of eternal generation where the scriptures spoke of the Son as the divine Word.

The Identity of the Word

Seventeenth and eighteenth-century England saw a rise in anti-Trinitarian theology that required constant attention. Gill first published directly on the Trinity in his aforementioned *The Doctrine of the Trinity, Stated and Vindicated*, in 1731. The spread of Sabellianism among Baptists formed the immediate context for its composition and publication.[15] This work provided a robust biblical and theological defense of the Trinity against both Sabellianism and Socinianism, both of which were common in the eighteenth century. With eye toward both of these Trinitarian heresies, Gill concentrated much of his efforts on the doctrine of the Son.[16] Out of nine chapters in this work, he devoted four to the second Person. In his first of these four chapters Gill introduced the identification of the second Person as the Word, referring to this designation as a "name, appellation, or character." Gill generally treated this identifier as a name that revealed particular

---

lifetime. For Gill, Trinitarian doctrines were not mere ideas. Rather, Gill viewed the doctrine of the Trinity as essential to the spiritual vitality of the church. Of its importance he wrote, "The doctrine of the Trinity is often represented as a speculative point, of no great moment whether it is believed or no, too mysterious and curious to be pryed into, and that it had better be let alone than meddled with; but alas! it enters into the whole of our salvation, and all the parts of it; into all the doctrines of the gospel, and into the experience of the saints; there is no doing without it." Gill, *Body of Doctrinal and Practical Divinity*, 138.

[15] John Rippon, *A Brief Memoir of the Life and Writings of the Late Rev. John Gill, D. D.* (1838 repr. Harrisonburg, VA: Sprinkle Publications, 2006), 37.

[16] In Gill's extended treatment of the personal distinctions between the Trinitarian Persons in Book I of his *Body of Doctrinal Divinity*, published at the end of his life, Gill would eventually consider eternal generation the *sine qua non* for maintaining Trinitarianism. John Gill, *Body of Doctrinal and Practical Divinity*, 142.

characteristics of the second person (to be described below). He believed the identification of the divine Person to whom this name belongs was easily determined in Scripture. In the writings of the apostle John, Gill noted that this is a frequent name given to the Son, which speaks to his deity, eternality, co-existence with the Father, and distinct personhood. Gill believed that the "Word" in John 1:14 was a clear reference to the Son. He highlighted the use of this name in John's other writings, including his first epistle (1 John 1:1; 5:7) and Revelation (1:2; 14:13). It is the second Person, the Son of God, who is also the Word of God.[17]

It was crucial to establish the meaning of this divine name since at least one highly influential author, Samuel Clarke (1675-1729), had incorporated it into his subordinationist Christology.[18] Gill, in his chapter on the Word or *Logos*, as well as in the relevant areas of his other writings, consistently incorporated the meaning of this divine name into his Trinitarianism. In doing so he articulated and

---

[17] John Gill, *The Doctrine of the Trinity*, 84–86. This same discussion can also be found in his sermon, "Paul's Farewell Discourse at Ephesus," on Acts 20:32. John Gill, *Sermons and Tracts*, 4:162–163. Very similar comments are also made in Gill's comments on John 1:1. John Gill, *Exposition of the Old and New Testaments*, 7:737.

[18] While Gill did not cite Clarke, or any other opponent on this point directly, it is likely that Gill had Clarke's or similar views in mind when he addressed this issue. It may also explain the reason he devoted an entire chapter to this divine name. Clarke rejected a Trinitarian understanding of the "Word" in John 1:1 as polytheism: "That the Word was Another Self-existent, Underived, Independent Person, co-ordinate to Him with whom he was: And This is the Impiety of Polytheism; subverting That First and Great Foundation of All Religion both Natural and Revealed, the Unity of GOD." Clarke instead argued that the Son is a person whose being was derived from the Father and who received "divine" attributes in a way unexplainable by human wisdom. He cited both Origen and Eusebius as authorities in his favor: "that the Word is a Person, deriving from the Father (with whom he existed before the World was,) both his Being it self, and incomprehensible Power and Knowledge, and other divine Attributes and Authority, in a Manner not revealed, and which humane Wisdome ought not to presume to be able to explain: And This is the Interpretation of the Learnedest and most Antient Writers in the Primitive Church." Samuel Clarke, *The Scripture-Doctrine of the Trinity: In Three Parts: Wherein All the Texts in the New Testament Relating to That Doctrine, and the Principle Passages in the Liturgy of the Church of England, Are Collected, Compared, and Explained* (London: James Knapton, 1712), 86, emphasis original.

defended the doctrine of the Trinity against the twin threats of Sabellianism and Socinianism.[19]

The Analogy of the Mind

Gill understood that the name, Word, or *Logos*, indicated something of the eternal nature of the Son. And like other theologians before him, he found the analogy of the mind helpful for achieving further understanding of the Son. For Gill, the Son is the *Logos* as the mental word, or thought of the mind. Like a thought is generated in the mind, so is Christ begotten of the Father. This analogy demonstrates not only that he was eternally with the Father, but that he is distinct from him. Deity, eternity, as well as distinct personality are all included in this name. In what may be his fullest expression of the analogy, Gill wrote,

> He may be so called, because As the mental word, or the conception of the mind, which is Λόγος ἐνδιάθετο, is the birth of the mind, begotten of it intellectually, and immaterially, without passion or motion; and is the very image and representation of the mind, and of the same nature with it, yet something distinct from it: So Christ is the begotten of the Father, the brightness of his glory, and the express image of his Person; of the same nature with him, though a Person distinct from him.[20]

There are four elements that come out of Gill's reflection of the Son as *Logos*: generation, image and representation, consubstantiality, and distinct personhood. From these elements, one can see how the analogy of the mind may prove fruitful for understanding eternal generation in the face of its anti-Trinitarian

---

[19] My assessment of Gill on this point has been illumined by Gilles Emery's work on Thomas Aquinas. See more below, specifically footnote 43.

[20] Gill, *Doctrine of the Trinity*, 101. See his similar explanations of this analogy in comments on John 1:1, Acts 20:32, and Hebrews 4:12 in Gill, *Exposition of the Old and New Testaments*, 7:737; 8:342; 9:396.

opposition. The analogy of the mind and thought provided another angle at which to behold this divine mystery. With respect to generation, the picture points away from physical, to spiritual generation, an understanding of generation which is more fitting to the nature of God as a divine Being.[21] Furthermore, the Son is described in other Scriptures as the "image" or "brightness" of the Father, providing additional ways of apprehending the Son's eternal nature (Col. 1:15, Heb. 1:3).[22]

Historical Use of the Analogy

Gill's use of the intellectual analogy for understanding this divine name was not unique to him, nor to other Reformed theologians. According to Herman Bavinck, the analogy was used by Justin Martyr, Tatian, Tertullian, Lacantius, and others. Bavinck wrote, "Athanasius and the Cappadocians regularly pictured generation as God's recognition of himself in his image, as the eternal utterance of a Word. The Father and the Son are related, they said, as mind (νους) is to word (λογος)." Bavinck continued to explain Augustine's attempt to find "clear imprints on the Trinity in human consciousness and reason."[23] Richard Muller

---

[21] This is a major part of Gill's argument and use of this analogy. Gill, *Body of Doctrinal and Practical Divinity*, 145. Gilles Emery's chapter, "The Person of the Son" (176-218), has been invaluable for understanding the significance of Gill's thought, especially on the use of the analogy as a way of understanding eternal generation. Much like Aquinas, Gill's theology of the Word helped him understand and communicate the nature of eternal generation. Gilles Emery, *The Trinitarian Theology of Saint Thomas Aquinas*, trans. Francesca Aran Murphy (Oxford: Oxford University Press, 2007), 178.

[22] I am indebted to Dr. Tyler Wittman for pointing me towards Thomas Aquinas and Gilles Emery as I sought to investigate Gill's use of the analogy of the mind. My conversations with Dr. Wittman have proved invaluable for understanding eternal generation and other related areas of inquiry. Additionally, Aquinas' condensed thoughts in this area can be found below. I am thankful also to Layne Hancock who originally pointed me to this book that has helped me better understand these issues. Thomas Aquinas, *Compendium of Theology*, trans. Richard J. Regan (Oxford: Oxford University Press, 2009), 35-39.

[23] Herman Bavinck, John Bolt, and John Vriend, *Reformed Dogmatics: God and Creation* (Grand Rapids: Baker Academic, 2004), 324-25.

characterizes William Perkins' use of the analogy for eternal generation as being a "medieval and specifically Thomist interpretation of the Son's procession as intellectual."[24] The importance of both Augustine and Aquinas with respect to the development of this doctrine is acknowledged by Gilles Emery: "Amongst the Fathers, it was St Augustine who particularly worked on pinpointing the nature of the 'word' within a theory of relation. Thomas' project can be seen as a personal development of this legacy. He puts forward his own viewpoint 'as following on from what Augustine has shown.'"[25] Aquinas' theology is of particular interest for understanding Gill, as Gill follows Aquinas' trajectory by using the analogy as a way of apprehending the eternal generation of the Son.[26]

Protestants in the reformation and post-reformation period were also not opposed to this analogy. Calvin, who was otherwise cautious with the use of analogies, nevertheless employed the analogy to explain this divine name in his commentary of John 1:1.[27] In addition to Calvin, Gill cited Antonius Walaeus (1573-

---

[24] Richard A. Muller, *Post-Reformation Reformed Dogmatics*, 4:313.

[25] Emery, *Trinitarian Theology of Aquinas*, 179.

[26] It is of note that while it is Aquinas who is credited with developing this theory, his work is rarely cited in the reformed documents that were accessed in this research. Additionally, I have yet to see a citation of Aquinas in my readings of Gill. I do not, however, believe this is because Gill did not read him. Gill appears to have owned a folio edition of Thomas' *Summa Theologiae*. With that said, it is likely that Gill's view, while downstream from Aquinas, was more immediately influenced by other Reformed orthodox theologians. *A Catalogue of the Library of the Late Reverend and Learned John Gill, D.D. Deceased. Comprehending a Fine Collection of Biblical and Oriental Literature;* (Cambridge: Unpublished manuscript, 1772), 9.

[27] "As to the Evangelist calling the Son of God the Speech, the simple reason appears to me to be, first, because he is the eternal Wisdom and Will of God; and, secondly, because he is the lively image of His purpose; for, as Speech is said to be among men the image of the mind, so it is not inappropriate to apply this to God, and to say that He reveals himself to us by his Speech." John Calvin, *Calvin's Commentaries* (Grand Rapids: Baker Books, 2009), 17: 26. Gill himself cited Calvin as holding to this view. Gill, *Sermons and Tracts*, 4:167, footnote q. Muller has documented Calvin's reticence to speculate about the Trinity from analogies in nature. Muller, *Post-Reformation Reformed Dogmatics*, 4:68–69.

1639) and Johann Heinrich Alsted (1588-1638) in support of this position.[28] Among English-speaking theologians whom Gill referenced in his writings, Edward Leigh (1602-1671) and Daniel Waterland (1683-1740) made use of the analogy. Describing eternal generation, Leigh wrote,

> In respect of this generation, the Sonne is called *The Word of the Father*, John 1.1. not a vanishing, but an essential word, because he is begotten of the Father, as the word from the mind. He is called *The Word of God*, both internal and conceived (that is, the Divine Understanding reflected upon it self from eternity, or God's knowledge of himself) so also he is the inward wisdom of God, *Prov.* 8. Because God knows himself as the first and most worthy object of contemplation, and external or uttered, which hath revealed the counsels of God to men, especially the elect; that we may know the Father by the Sonne as it were by an Image, *John* 1.18. so also he is the externall wisdome instructing us concerning the Will and Wisdome of the Father to Salvation.[29]

Similarly, Waterland stated the following in a sermon on John 1:1: "But I must observe, that the Greek Λόγος, which we render WORD, may signify either *inward* Thought, or *outward* Speech. And it has with good reason been supposed by the *Catholick* Writers, that the design of this Name was to intimate that the Relation of Father and Son, bears some Resemblance and Analogy to that of *Thought*, or of *Speech* to the Mind."[30] Thus, when Gill

---

[28] He additionally cited a "Theophilacti," whom I understand to be Theophylact of Ohrid (1055-1107). Gill, *Sermons and Tracts*, 4:167.

[29] Edward Leigh, *A Systeme or Body of Divinity: Consisting of Ten Books. Wherein the Fundamentals and Mina Grounds of Religion Are Opened; the Contrary Errours Refuted; Most of the Controversies Between Us, the Papists, Arminians and Socinians Discussed and Handled; Several Scriptures Explained, and Vindicated from Corrupt Glosses.*, 2nd ed. (London: A.M for William Lee, 1662), 264, emphasis original.

[30] Dan. Waterland, *Eight Sermons Preach'd at the Cathedral Church of St. Paul, in Defense of the Divinity of Our Lord Jesus Christ; Upon the Encouragement given by the*

conceived of the Son as the Word in this manner, he did so following the precedent of the Reformed and broader Christian tradition.

The Begotten Word

Gill explicitly connected the Word with eternal generation in his explanation of the intellectual analogy provided in his *The Doctrine of the Trinity*.[31] According to Gill, the Son is the "mental word, or the conception of the mind," which is "the birth of the mind."[32] This birth, or generation is to be thought of in a particular way in keeping with the nature of the subject.[33] Thus, as the "mental word ... is the birth of the mind, begotten of it intellectually, and immaterially, without passion or motion ... So Christ is the begotten of the Father."[34] This connection reveals that the name, Word, is closely tied to the name, Son, since it is the Son's generation that is intended by the use of the name, Word. This name, as Gill understood it, helped explain the nature of the Son's eternal generation. Thus, this divine name finds importance as it explains a fundamental doctrine of the Christian religion. In Gill's mind, the doctrine of eternal generation was indispensable, as it provided the foundation not only for the Son's deity, but was *the* means of explaining the distinction of Persons within the divine essence.[35]

The importance of this name appeared in Gill's *Body of Doctrinal Divinity*, where he gave his most detailed exposition and

---

Lady Moyer, and at the Appointment of the Ld. Bishop of London. (Cambridge: London, 1720), 5, emphasis original.

[31] For support of this doctrine, Gill cited Ignatius, Athenagoras, Theophilus, and Tatian. Gill, *Doctrine of the Trinity*, 101. Godet provides references to modern editions of these authors' works cited by Gill cites. Steven Tshombe Godet, "The Trinitarian Theology of John Gill (1697–1771)," 175.

[32] Gill, *Doctrine of the Trinity*, 101.

[33] See Gill, *Body of Doctrinal and Practical Divinity*, 145.

[34] Gill, *Doctrine of the Trinity*, 101.

[35] Gill, *Body of Doctrinal and Practical Divinity*, 143–144.

In Essence One, in Persons Three

defense of eternal generation.[36] In these pages, Gill defended eternal generation against Socinian objections. He approached the discussion from various angles, but explained that divine generation must be understood in a way that is reflective of God's divine, spiritual nature:

> When Scriptures ascribe generation to the Divine Being, it must be understood in a manner suitable to it, and not of carnal and corporal generation; no man in his senses can ever think that God generates as man does; nor believe that ever any man held such a notion of generation in God.[37]

Gill thus removed misguided notions of the Father's relation to the Son through generation and made way for a proper understanding of the Son's eternal generation from the Father. After producing a citation of Socinus in which he accused "Evangelics" of holding to a view in which God generates "one like himself ... as animals do," Gill demonstrated his own approach: "But generation must be understood of such generation as agrees with the nature of a spirit, and of an infinite uncreated spirit, as God is."[38] It is at this point that Gill began to rely upon the analogy of the mind, drawn from the meaning of the Son's identification as *Logos*. Additionally, it is at this point where Thomas Aquinas's theology of the Word may help to illustrate Gill's use of the analogy. Gilles Emery explains Aquinas' theology of the Word in this way:

> The Word is a person who subsists in himself, distinct from the Father from whom he proceeds; being equal to, and of the same nature as, the Father, he is the perfect expression and presentation of the Father. The notion of *Word* also enables one to grasp what it means for God to be Son, using an

---

[36] See Gill, *Body of Doctrinal and Practical Divinity*, 143–159.
[37] Gill, *Body of Doctrinal and Practical Divinity*, 145.
[38] Gill, *Body of Doctrinal and Practical Divinity*, 145.

analogy which is adapted to the spiritual nature of God. To put it another way, it is the notion of the *Word* which, according to St Thomas, gives one an understanding of *begetting the Son* which is best fitted to God.[39]

Consonant with Emery's assessment of Aquinas, it may be said of Gill that he considered the name, Word, and the analogy that is signaled by it, to be a helpful means of understanding eternal generation in a way that rightly accords with the Son's divine nature. Gill produced an additional example to further the analogy entailed in this name when he wrote, "that spirits generate we know from the souls or spirits we have about us and in us; our minds, which are spirits, generate thought; thought is the *conception*, and *birth* of the mind; and so we speak of it in common and ordinary speech, *I conceive*, or such a man *conceives* so and so." This illustration of the relation between a thought to the mind corresponds with the coexistence, distinction of Persons in the Godhead, and of the relation of Father and Son in generation: "now as soon as the mind is, thought is, they commence together and they co-exist, and always will; and this the mind begets within itself; without any mutation or alterations in itself." The internal and immaterial nature of generation is thus given shape by the analogy of the mind, to which this divine name points. As Gill penned it, "the mind to God who is Νους, the eternal mind, to Christ, the eternal Λογος, word and wisdom of God; who is in some sort represented by λογος ενδιαθετος, the internal mental word." Gill provided further explanation of these analogies, quoting both Plato and Aristotle before concluding the discussion. The Son, who is the Word of God, is begotten from eternity. This biblical affirmation, however, does not mean that there was ever a time the Son was not.

---

[39] With respect to this name, Emery's entire chapter is illuminating (pp. 176–218). According to him, Aquinas' "doctrine of the Word is incontestably the heart of Thomas' Trinitarian theology" (p. 179). Emery, *Trinitarian Theology of Aquinas*, 189, emphasis original.

Nor does it mean that the Son is a created being—he is of the very same essence as God. All of this, Gill asserted, can be proved by this analogy, indicated by the Son's identification as the Word:

> Now if our finite created spirits, or minds, are capable of generating thought, the internal word or speech, and that without any motion, change or alteration, without any diminution and corruption, without division of their nature or multiplication of their essence; then in an infinitely more perfect manner can God, an infinite uncreated spirit, beget his Son, the eternal Word, wisdom, reason, and understanding, in his eternal mind, which he never was without, nor was he before it.[40]

Gill expressed the purpose for explaining this divine name: "these things considered, may serve in some measure to relieve our minds, and make it more easy to us to conceive of this wonderful and mysterious affair."[41] Gill quoted Amandus Polanus (1561–1610) at length to further demonstrate how the analogy connects to eternal generation:

> Mental or metaphysical generation ... is a similitude and adumbration of divine generation; as the mind begets by nature, not by power, so likewise God; as the mind begets a birth simple and perfect, so God; as the mind begets immutably (or without mutation) so God; as the mind begets of itself in itself, so God; as the mind does not beget out of matter without itself, so neither God, as the mind always begets and cannot but beget, so God the Father; as metaphysical generation abides, so the divine.[42]

---

[40] Gill, *Body of Doctrinal and Practical Divinity*, 145–146.

[41] Gill, *Body of Doctrinal and Practical Divinity*, 146.

[42] Gill cited Polanus' *Syntagma Theologiae Christianae* (1615), 204. Gill, *Body of Doctrinal and Practical Divinity*, 146.

Jonathan E. Swan

In Gill's theology, the identity of the Son as the eternal *Logos* helped explain the nature of eternal generation against rival theologies. Contrary to Socinianism, the analogy of the mind provided Gill a means of understanding the Son's eternal generation that upheld the Son's eternal co-existence with the Father, his consubstantiality; and, contrary to Sabellianism, personal distinction between the Persons of the Trinity.[43]

The Image of God

As the Son is the Word, he is also the image of the Father and the brightness of his glory. Gill tied this language from Hebrews 1:3 and Colossians 1:15 to the analogy of the mind explicitly as mutually defining aspects of the Word. Gill's interpretation of these texts, then, further illumined his theology of the Word, particularly as it related to the analogy of the mind.

In Gill's understanding of Hebrews 1:3, being both the image and the brightness of the Father says much of the same with respect of the Word—that he is coessential (consubstantial) with the Father but is a distinct person from him. With respect to the analogy of the mind, the Word that proceeds by birth from the mind is the brightness of it. Particularly, the Son is the brightness of the Father. By this Gill believed the Scriptures pointed to the consubstantial nature of both the Father and the Son. It is all the glorious perfections of the Father that the Son shines forth. Being the brightness of the Father's glory with respect to the divine essence, "he has the same glorious nature and perfection, and the same glorious names, as Jehovah, the Lord of glory, &c. and the same glory, homage, and worship is given him." Seeking to further tease

---

[43] The way in which Aquinas' theology of the Word functioned to ward off both Arianism and Sabellianism, which at root is the same as Gill on this point, is summarized here: Emery, *Trinitarian Theology of Aquinas*, 188. Again, Emery's outline of Aquinas' theology was influential in helping me see these ideas and their function in Gill.

out the significance of the imagery of the sun—which points to the Father and Son's consubstantiality and personal distinction—he wrote,

> the allusion is to the sun, and its beam or ray: so some render it *the ray of his glory*; and may lead us to observe, that the Father and the Son are of the same nature, as the sun and its ray; and that the one is not before the other, and yet distinct from each other, and cannot be divided or separated one from another.

The concurrence with the mind analogy can hardly be missed. Although adding to the analogy with the imagery of the Son shining forth the Father's glory like a ray of sunlight from the sun, the import of this imagery leads to the same conclusions—that the Father and Son both exist together from eternity, share the same essence, and yet are personally distinct.[44]

The revelation of the Word as the brightness of the Father's glory provided another analogy, or imagery, for understanding eternal generation. Immediately following Gill's discussion in the *Body of Divinity* regarding the analogy of the mind as a means of understanding eternal generation, Gill enlisted the imagery of the sun, taken from Hebrews 1:3, to help illumine the doctrine of eternal generation. His conclusions are the same with this analogy as they are with that of the mind:

> To this may be added another similitude, which may help us in this matter, and serve to illustrate it; and that is the sun, to which God is sometimes compared; the sun generates its own ray of light, without any change, corruption, division, and diminution; it never was without its ray of light, as it

---

[44] At this point in his exposition, Gill cross-referenced the Chaldee paraphrases as using the phrase, "the brightness of his glory," and pointed his readers to Wisdom 7:26. Gill, *Exposition of the Old and New Testaments*, 9:375, emphasis original.

must have been had it been prior to it; they commenced together and co-exist, and will as long as the sun endures; and to this there seems to be an allusion, when Christ is called the *brightness*, απαυγασμα, the effulgence, the beaming forth *of his Father's glory*, Heb. i.3.⁴⁵

Commenting on the author of Hebrews' reference to the Son as God's image, Gill stated that the Scriptures' revelation of Christ as the image of the Father means also that he has "equality and sameness of nature, and distinction of persons." Gill quickly explained how: "for if the Father is God, Christ must be so too; and if he is a person, his Son must be so likewise, or he can't be the express image and character of him." Having again connected this analogy to the doctrines of consubstantiality and personal distinction, Gill referred the reader to his note on Colossians 1:15, where this imagery was explained further, and where it was also connected to the Son's identification as Word.⁴⁶ In his interpretation of this text Gill explained that the Son is the image of the Father—not deity. And he is so as the Son of God. This led Gill to conclude that rather than existing as a different substance that provides a "shadow" of the Father, it points to their equality, consubstantiality, and distinction within the divine nature:⁴⁷

> [he] is the natural, essential, and eternal image of his father, an increated one, perfect and complete, and in which he takes infinite complacency and delight: this designs more than a shadow and representation, or than bare similitude and likeness; it includes sameness of nature and perfections; ascertains the personality of the son, his distinction from the father, whose image he is; and yet implies no inferiority,

---

⁴⁵ Gill, *Body of Doctrinal and Practical Divinity*, 146, emphasis original.
⁴⁶ Gill, *Exposition of the Old and New Testaments*, 9:375.
⁴⁷ Gill, *Exposition of the Old and New Testaments*, 9:171-172.

as the following verses clearly shew, since all that the gather hath are his.[48]

This description, Gill remarked, was consonant with Philo's writings about the *Logos*, whom he says is the image of God.[49]

The above discussion of these texts reveals a close connection between the Son as Word and Image. This close conceptual and linguistic connection between Gill's discussion of the mind analogy and his exegesis of Hebrews 1:3 and Colossians 1:15 demonstrate how Gill understood the meaning of the Son's identification as the *Logos* by way of the mind analogy, but also how he explained the nature of the Son's eternal generation by pointing to other biblical similes and analogies that speak to the same thing. Gill understood that the Scripture's images and analogies all come together to help Christians understand the person and nature of the Son. Gill used both the analogy of the mind and the sun to assist the Christian's knowledge of the Son's eternal generation, which is the Son's defining and "distinctive relative property" in the Godhead.[50] Neither analogies were arbitrarily chosen based on what Gill found suitable to explain the Son's eternal generation. Gill specifically mentioned that the sun similitude was alluded to in Hebrews 1:3 by the word "brightness."[51] Far from a mere rational speculation on the nature of the divine essence and persons, Gill's use of these similes was the product of grammatical, historical, analogical, and theological exegesis by which every text was interpreted in its full canonical context.

---

[48] Gill also stated that this could refer to his office as Mediator, "in whom, as such is a most glorious display of the love, grace, and mercy of God, of his holiness and righteousness, of his truth and faithfulness, and of his power and wisdom." Gill, 9:172.

[49] Gill, *Exposition of the Old and New Testaments*, 9:172.

[50] Gill, *Body of Doctrinal and Practical Divinity*, 143–44. Similarly, Emery notes that it is the "relation of origin" that is "uncovered in the divine Word." Emery, *Trinitarian Theology of Aquinas*, 188.

[51] Gill, *Body of Doctrinal and Practical Divinity*, 146.

Jonathan E. Swan

The Wisdom of God

Connected to the Son as the Word of God is the consideration of him as the Wisdom of God.[52] Often in Gill's writings, the two names are mentioned together.[53] Considering the metaphor of the mind, it would make sense that the thought or conception of the mind would also be considered its wisdom. Gill understood references to God's wisdom in two ways—personally and essentially. Personally, it applies to the second Person. Essentially, it applies to the divine essence as an essential attribute shared by all divine Persons. In his *Body of Doctrinal Divinity*, Gill considered wisdom as an essential attribute of the divine nature.[54] In other places, such as his exposition of Proverbs 1 and 8, he considered it with respect to the Son personally.[55] The connection between God's wisdom, the divine Word, and the analogy of the mind, was made explicit in Gill's *Body of Doctrinal Divinity* when he tied both "word and wisdom of God" to the "internal mental word" represented by the *Logos*.[56]

The identification of the Son as Wisdom was made explicit in Gill's exegesis of Proverbs. He wrote that Wisdom is best thought of in Proverbs as referring to the Son. This designation speaks "of the consummate and perfect wisdom that is in him." Gill applied this designation to the Son in various respects, such as his mediatorial office and his incarnation. Identifying "wisdom" in Proverbs 1:20 with the Son, he referred to wisdom as "a divine Person," immediately invoking the name "*Logos*," or "Word."[57] In Proverbs 8:22, Gill further clarified that the Wisdom of God was

---

[52] Recall also the quotations from Calvin and Leigh above.

[53] While there are more, these examples will suffice. Gill, *Body of Doctrinal and Practical Divinity*, 145, 252. Gill, *Exposition of the Old and New Testaments*, 4:333, 349, 382; 7:741.

[54] Gill, *Body of Doctrinal and Practical Divinity*, 64–70.

[55] See especially his commentary on Proverbs, specifically his comments on Proverbs 1:20. Gill, *Exposition of the Old and New Testaments*, 4:333.

[56] Gill, *Body of Doctrinal and Practical Divinity*, 145.

[57] Gill, *Exposition of the Old and New Testaments*, 4:333, emphasis original.

possessed by God "in right of paternity." This verse, used by Arius (according to Gill) to prove the Son was created, was interpreted by Gill as a reference to eternal generation. According to Gill, the Wisdom of God has eternally existing with God as the Father's Wisdom and is the Creator of the universe. He commented that this verse

> denotes the Lord's having, possessing, and enjoying his word and wisdom as his own proper son; which possession of him is expressed by his being with him and in him, and in his bosom, and as one brought forth and brought up by him ... when he went forth in his wisdom and power, and created all things; then he did possess his son, and made us of him; for by him he made the worlds.[58]

Gill teased out the implications of Proverbs 8:22: "This shews the real and actual existence of Christ from eternity, his relation to Jehovah his Father, his nearness to him, equality with him, and distinctions from him."[59] This name, given in Scripture to the Son, provided yet another way of understanding the relation of the Father and Son in eternal generation and divine action: the Word is the Wisdom of the Father begotten from all eternity.[60]

Gill's Initial Objection to the Analogy

While in much of Gill's *Exposition*, and especially in his *Body of Doctrinal Divinity*, he made use of the analogy of the mind when considering the divine Word, it appears that he was not always so comfortable with it. In his sermon, *Paul's Farwel Address at Ephesus*, he provided an near-identical description of the analogy which appeared in the *Doctrine of the Trinity*, but then argued that

---

[58] Gill, *Exposition of the Old and New Testaments*, 4:382.

[59] Gill, *Exposition of the Old and New Testaments*, 4:383.

[60] See Gill's comments on Proverbs 8:22-24, Gill, *Exposition of the Old and New Testaments*, 382-383.

this understanding of the name may be too speculative to be useful:

> But this [the analogy of the mind] may be thought too curious, and as falling short (as all things else in nature do) of expressing that adorable mystery of godliness. And, indeed, oftentimes, when we indulge our own curiosity, and give a loose to our thoughts this way, we run into confusion, and every evil work. For though Christ is certainly and really God, as well as man; yet I am afraid that our abstracted ideas of him, as God, of his Generation and Sonship, distinct from him, as Mediator, often lead us into labyrinths, and draw off our minds from the principle things we have in view. God having set bounds around his inscrutable and incomprehensible Deity, as he ordered to be set about mount Sinai, when he descended on it; that we may not too curiously gaze upon it, and perish. It seems to be his will, that our saving knowledge of him, and converse with him, should be all in and through Christ the glorious Mediator. With this we should be contented. It is enough for us, that this Divine Person, who is called λογος, *the Word*, is God; for John expresses it in so many words.[61]

Having made this argument, Gill followed by stating that he believed the Son is called Word because of his work in the economy of salvation.[62]

For these reasons, Gill was uncomfortable with the analogy for the mind as an explanation of this appellation. But, by the time this sermon was incorporated into the *Doctrine of the Trinity*, Gill elided the qualifying statement and put the analogy forth as a

---

[61] Gill, *Sermons and Tracts*, 4:167-168, emphasis original.

[62] Gill, *Sermons and Tracts,* 4:168-171. Gill cited a Targum of Hosea 1:7 as proof that the Son is called Word in this sense. He then outlined four ways in which the Son acts as Word in the economy of salvation. First, he spoke in the eternal council and covenant; second, he spoke creation into existence; third, he knows and speaks the mind of the Father; fourth, he speaks as an advocate for his people in heaven's court.

reason for the divine name. It is, in fact, the first reason he gives. While there is no explicit reason given for this change of heart, Gill's use of the analogy as an explanation for eternal generation, which he reaffirmed later in his *Body of Doctrinal Divinity*, may provide a clue. It is likely, considering the enormous pressure of anti-Trinitarianism in England, that Gill was pressed to see the fruitfulness of this analogy for understanding, explaining, and defending the nature of the eternal Son.

Exegetical Underpinnings from John 1

While the analogy of the mind, derived from the divine Word, is laden with significance, it arose in Gill's theology as a product of exegetical and theological reflection. Gill's understanding of the divine Word drew heavily from the Prologue of John's Gospel, where the divine *Logos* prominently appears.[63] Gill stated at the opening of his chapter on the divine Word that John 1:1–2 proves his deity, eternality, co-existence with the Father, and distinct personhood—all realities included in the analogy of the mind.[64] These realities are given shape and significance as they are further revealed in the Prologue of John.[65]

---

[63] With respect to teasing out the meaning of the mind analogy, Gill's commentary does far less than Aquinas' commentary on the same book. Nevertheless, Gill's exegesis supports the primary doctrinal assertions that he attributes to the analogy. Emery, *Trinitarian Theology of Aquinas*, 178, 183–185. This key section in Aquinas' first lecture on the John 1:1–2 provides a clear treatment of the *Logos*. Thomas Aquinas, *Commentary on the Gospel of John: Chapters 1–8*, ed. Aquinas Institute, trans. Fabian R. Larcher, *Latin/English Edition of the Works of St. Thomas Aquinas*, vol. 35 (Lander, WY: Aquinas Institute for the Study of Sacred Doctrine, 2013), 12–16 [C.1, L1, 25–32].

[64] Gill, *Doctrine of the Trinity*, 85.

[65] For an introduction into the ways the Gospel of John was used in the midst of Trinitarian debates in Early Modern England, see Paul Lim's helpful chapter in Paul C.H. Lim, *Mystery Unveiled: The Crisis of the Trinity in Early Modern England* (Oxford: Oxford University Press: 2012), 271–319. Lim points out the importance of John in debates about the Trinity: "The Gospel of John played a formative role in the Christological controversies of both the patristic and the Reformation periods; thus, it comes as little surprise that considerable scholarly attention has been given to its *Wirkungsgeschichte*." Lim, *Mystery Unveiled*, 271–272.

Gill took the opportunity when interpreting the very first phrase of John 1:1 to explain how it refers to the Son, the essential word, and for what reasons. He is the essential Word, Gill reasoned, on account of his being the eternal Son, begotten from eternity as a thought is in the mind. He is also called Word on account of his actions and by his being "the interpreter of his father's mind."[66] Gill asserted that by "beginning" (1:1), the apostle John speaks of eternity. As he was in the beginning, he was with God. Here Gill highlighted the personal distinction, but also the consubstantial nature of the Father and Son:

> but this phrase denotes the existence of the word with the father, his relation and nearness to him, his equality with him, and particularly the distinction of his person from him, as well as his eternal being with him; for he was always with him, and is, and ever will be.[67]

Gill expounded the full deity of Christ by commenting on John's statement that "*the word was God*":

> not made a God, as he is said hereafter to be made flesh; nor constituted or appointed a God, or a God by office; but truly and properly God, in the highest sense of the word, as appears from the names by which he is called; as Jehovah, God, our, your, their, and my God, God with us, the mighty God, God over all, the great God, the living God, the true God, and eternal life; and from his perfections, and the whole fulness of the Godhead that dwells in him, as independence, eternity, immutability, omniscience, and omnipotence.[68]

---

[66] Gill, *Exposition of the Old and New Testaments*, 7:737.

[67] Gill, *Exposition of the Old and New Testaments*, 7:738.

[68] Gill, *Exposition of the Old and New Testaments*, 7:738-739, Gill's translation, emphasis original.

In Essence One, in Persons Three

Adding to these comments the Son's works and the "worship given [to] him," Gill argued for the divinity of the Word from John 1:1. The deity of Christ is also substantiated, according to Gill, by the Apostle's statement in John 1:4, that *in him was life* (Gill's translation, italics original). Gill argued that "life" points to two things. First, the "divine life" that the Son has in himself (*autotheos*), and also the life that he communicates to others. In a likely reference to Job 19:25, Gill correlated this text with Job's understanding of the Word "as his living redeemer." This statement, Gill continued, "regards him as the word and living God, and distinguishes him from the written Word, and shews that he is not a mere idea in the divine mind, but a truly divine Person."[69]

The divine Word who has life is also the light and the giver of light. It is the divine life of the second Person through which men receive their capacity to perceive as rational beings. Gill identified the creating power of the living Word when he wrote, "for when Christ, the word, breathed into man the breath of life, and he became a living soul, he filled him with rational light and knowledge." For Gill, this proved the divinity of the Word. He went on to argue that all "spiritual and supernatural light," by which people are saved, sanctified, and glorified, is from Christ. Gill connected the "light of men" (John 1:4) to the light spoken of in John 1:7, whom he identified as Christ: "by which is meant, not the light of nature, or reason; nor the light of the Gospel: but Christ himself, the author of light, natural, spiritual, and eternal."[70] This identification is further supported, in Gill's estimation, by appeals to both the Old Testament and Philo, who connected this name to the *Logos*.[71]

While the above only samples Gill's *Exposition* of John's Prologue, these few passages highlight Gill's understanding of the

---

[69] Gill, *Exposition of the Old and New Testaments*, 7:740.
[70] Gill, *Exposition of the Old and New Testaments*, 7:740–741.
[71] Gill, *Exposition of the Old and New Testaments*, 7:741.

essential characteristics of the divine Word, namely, his deity, eternality, co-existence with the Father, and distinct personality.

Conclusion

In this brief overview I have argued that John Gill believed eternal generation was essential for understanding the personal distinctions between the Trinitarian Persons yet without conceiving of these distinctions as entailing a communication of essence. I have also argued that Gill took cues from both the broader Christian tradition, as well as Reformed sources, as he understood the Scriptures' designation of the Son as the divine Word to produce an analogy of the mind that coincided with other Scriptural images and names to provide further understanding of the Son's eternal generation.

5
"Co-equal, co-essential, and co-eternal": Anne Dutton on the Trinity

Michael A.G. Haykin

With the passing of the Act of Toleration on May 24, 1689, religious liberty was guaranteed for various communities outside of the Anglican state church such as the Congregationalists and Particular Baptists, and a religious pluralism was enshrined within the make-up of English society. The Act did not provide such liberty for Anti-Trinitarians, though, as we have seen, the following decade of the 1690s saw the beginning of a profound Trinitarian controversy that raged on and off throughout the "long" eighteenth century. Contrary to the impression given by various recent historical overviews of the doctrine of the Trinity, the late seventeenth and eighteenth centuries were actually replete with critical battles over Trinitarianism.[1]

Now, a number of key Particular Baptist authors like John Gill (1697–1771), Caleb Evans (1737–1791), and Andrew Fuller (1754–1815), were deeply involved in this controversy about God's being and penned significant treatises in defence of his Triunity. However, one Particular Baptist author, who also wrote on this subject and who has been generally overlooked, is Anne Dutton (1692–1765). Following an introduction to Dutton's life and writing, this chapter will focus on her discussion of Trinitarian ontology in her tract *A Letter on the Divine Eternal Sonship of Jesus Christ: As the Second Person in the Ever-blessed Three-one God* (1757), written in

---

[1] For an exception, see Stephen R. Holmes, *The Quest for the Trinity: The Doctrine of God in Scripture, History, and Modernity* (Downers Grove, IL: IVP Academic, 2012), 170–181.

response to a work by the Anglican Evangelical William Romaine (1714–1795).²

Introducing Anne Dutton

Anne Dutton was born Anne Williams to godly Congregationalist parents in 1692 in Northampton, the East Midlands.³ Her conversion came at the age of thirteen after a serious illness.⁴ Two years later, in 1707, she joined the Congregationalist church, although she wrestled with doubt and various fears as a young believer. Subsequently, though, she experienced a significant encounter with the Holy Spirit that she interpreted as the sealing of the Spirit—a phrase derived from such Pauline texts as Ephesians 1:13 and 4:30. As she later recalled the experience, the Spirit used Philippians 4:4 ("Rejoice in the Lord always: and again I say rejoice," KJV) in his sealing of her heart:

> [This] Word brake in ... upon my heart, with such a ray of glorious light, that directed my soul to the true and proper object of its joy, even the Lord himself. I was pointed thereto, as with a finger: In the *Lord*, not in your *frames*. *In* the Lord, not in what you enjoy *from* him, but in what you are in *him*. And the Lord seal'd my instruction, and fill'd my heart brim-full of joy, in the faith of my eternal interest, and unchangeable standing in *him*; and of *his* being an

---

² Anne Dutton, *A Letter on the Divine Eternal Sonship of Jesus Christ: As the Second Person in the Ever-blessed Three-one God* (London: J. Hart, 1757).

³ For Dutton's life and thought, see especially J. C. Whitebrook, "The Life and Works of Mrs. Ann Dutton," *Transactions of the Baptist Historical Society* 7, nos. 3–4 (1921): 129–146; Stephen J. Stein, "A Note on Anne Dutton, Eighteenth-Century Evangelical," *Church History* 44 (1975): 485–491; Michael D. Sciretti, Jr., " 'Feed My Lambs': The Spiritual Direction Ministry of Calvinistic British Baptist Anne Dutton During the Early Years of the Evangelical Revival" (PhD thesis, Baylor University, 2009).

The sketch of her early life that follows is dependent in part on Sciretti, "Feed My Lambs," 48–115. For her own account of her conversion, which she detailed in her *A Brief Account of the Gracious Dealings of God, with a Poor, Sinful, Unworthy Creature* (1743), see Watson, comp., *Selected Spiritual Writings of Anne Dutton*, 3:8–27.

⁴ Sciretti, "Feed My Lambs," 51–53.

infinite fountain of blessedness, for me to rejoice in alway; even when the streams of sensible enjoyments fail'd. Thus the Blessed Spirit took me by the arms, and taught me to go.

... the Lord the Spirit went on to reveal Christ more and more to me, as the great foundation of my faith and joy. He shew'd me my everlasting standing in his person, grace and righteousness: and gave me to see my security in his unchangeableness, under all the changes which pass'd over me. And then I began to rejoice in my dear Lord Jesus, as always the *same*, even when my frames *alter'd*.[5]

In other words, Dutton learned to put her faith in Christ alone, and not in her experience of him. Her beliefs about the sealing of the Spirit were probably derived from reading the works of the Puritan Thomas Goodwin (1600–1679).[6]

In 1710, she transferred her church affiliation to an open-membership Baptist church in Northampton, pastored at the time by John Moore (1662–1726).[7] There, in her words, she found "fat, green pastures," for, as she went on to explain, "Mr. Moore was a great doctrinal preacher: and the special advantage I receiv'd under his ministry, was the establishment of my judgment in the doctrines of the gospel."[8] It was in this congregation that she was baptized as a believer around 1713.[9]

When she was twenty-two in 1715, she married a Thomas Cattell, and moved with her husband to London. While there she worshipped with the Particular Baptist church that met at premises

---

[5] Dutton, *A Brief Account of the Gracious Dealings of God* in Watson, comp., *Selected Spiritual Writings of Anne Dutton*, 3:27-28. I have modernized Dutton's capitalization of words in her writings, which Watson retained.

[6] On Goodwin's influence on Dutton, see Sciretti, "Feed My Lambs," 62.

[7] On Moore, see Sciretti, "Feed My Lambs," 59-60, n.42.

[8] Dutton, *A Brief Account of the Gracious Dealings of God* in Watson, comp., *Selected Spiritual Writings of Anne Dutton*, 3:47, 50.

[9] Sciretti, "Feed My Lambs," 64-65.

on Wood Street in the Cripplegate region.[10] Founded by Hanserd Knollys (1599-1691), this work had known some rough times in the days immediately prior to Dutton's coming to the church. David Crosley (1670-1744), an evangelist from the Pennine hills in Northern England, had been the pastor of the work from 1705 to 1709, but he had been disfellowshipped for drunkenness, unchaste conduct with women, and lying to the church about these matters when accused.[11] The sorrow and sense of betrayal, disappointment and consternation in the church would have run deep. It was not until 1714 that the church succeeded in finding a new pastor. John Skepp (d.1721), a member of the Cambridge Congregationalist church of Joseph Hussey (1659-1726), was called that year to be the pastor.

Now, Hussey is often seen as the father of eighteenth-century High Calvinism, insomuch as he argued in his book *God's Operations of Grace but no Offers of Grace* (1707) that offering Christ indiscriminately to sinners is something that smacks of "creature-co-operation and creature-concurrence" in the work of salvation. Skepp published but one book, and that posthumously, which was entitled *Divine Energy: or The Efficacious Operations of the Spirit of God upon the Soul of Man* (1722). In it he appears to have followed Hussey's approach to evangelism. It is sometimes argued that Anne Dutton's exposure to High Calvinism at a young age shaped

---

[10] On this church's history during this period, see Murdina D. MacDonald, "London Calvinistic Baptists 1689-1727: Tensions within a Dissenting Community under Toleration" (DPhil thesis, Regent's Park College, Oxford, 1982), 109-131.

[11] For his story, see the small study by B. A. Ramsbottom, *The Puritan Samson: The Life of David Crosley 1669-1744* (Harpenden, Hertfordshire: Gospel Standard Trust Publications, 1991). See also details in MacDonald, "London Calvinistic Baptists 1689-1727," 118-119. Crosley genuinely repented, and years later, having lived a life in accord with genuine repentance, he would know some usefulness again in the Lord's work. He carried on a correspondence with George Whitefield, who noted that their "sentiments as the essential doctrines of the gospel, exactly harmonize[d]" and who wrote a commendatory preface for a sermon Crosley published on Samson. See George Whitefield, "Preface to the Reader" in David Crosley, *Samson a Type of Christ* (London 1744 ed.; repr. Newburyport, MA: William Barrett, 1796), iii.

her thinking for the rest of her life. If so, it is curious to find her rejoicing in the ministry of free-offer preachers like George Whitefield (1714–1770) in later years.

Skepp, though, was an impressive preacher, owing in part to what Dutton called his "quickness of thought, aptness of expression, suitable affection, and a most agreeable delivery."[12] Despite his refusal to freely offer the gospel to all and sundry, the overall trend in the church during his ministry was one of growth. There were 179 members when he came as pastor in 1714. When he died in 1721, the church's membership had grown to 212.[13]

In the early months of 1719, though, Dutton's life underwent a deep trial as her husband of but five or six years died.[14] She returned to her family in Northampton, and found herself wrestling with spiritual depression. In her words, Dutton sought God "in his ordinances, in one place and another; but alas! I found him not."[15] She was not long single, however. A second marriage in the middle months of 1720 was to Benjamin Dutton (1691–1747), a clothier who had studied for vocational ministry in various places, among them Glasgow University. Anne and Benjamin had met in the final months of 1719 and within a year they were wed.[16]

Ministry took the couple to such towns as Whittlesey and Wisbech in Cambridgeshire, before leading them finally in 1731 to a Particular Baptist congregation in Great Gransden, Huntingdonshire, in 1733.[17] It is noteworthy that prior to this call to Great Gransden, Benjamin Dutton had wrestled with alcoholism. But

---

[12] Dutton, *A Brief Account of the Gracious Dealings of God* in Watson, comp., *Selected Spiritual Writings of Anne Dutton*, 3:51.

[13] MacDonald, "London Calvinistic Baptists 1689-1727," 124.

[14] Dutton, *A Brief Account of the Gracious Dealings of God* in Watson, comp., *Selected Spiritual Writings of Anne Dutton*, 3:63-64.

[15] Dutton, *A Brief Account of the Gracious Dealings of God* in Watson, comp., *Selected Spiritual Writings of Anne Dutton*, 3:70.

[16] Sciretti, "Feed My Lambs," 76-77.

[17] For a brief history of the church, see Joseph Ivimey, *A History of the English Baptists* (London: Isaac Taylor Hinston and Holdsworth & Ball, 1830), 4:509-510.

the Lord delivered him completely around the time of the move to Great Gransden. In his own words, he said that he now "stood not in need of wine, or strong drink. The Lord also, of his great goodness, took away my *inclination* thereto; so that I had no more inclination to it, or desire after it, than if I had never tasted any in my whole life."[18]

Under Benjamin Dutton's preaching the church flourished so that on any given Sunday the congregation numbered anywhere between 250 and 350, of whom roughly 50 were members. This growth led to the building of a new meeting-house, which can still be seen in the village. Benjamin decided to go to America to help raise funds to pay off the debt incurred in the building of the meeting-house but the ship on which he was returning foundered not far from the British coast in 1747, and Dutton was drowned. He had sent the money he had raised by means of another ship, however, so that at least was not lost.

"A talent for writing"

Widowed now for the second time, Anne Dutton was to live another eighteen years. During that time "the fame of her ... piety," as Baptist historian Joseph Ivimey (1773–1834) once referred to her spirituality,[19] became known in Evangelical circles on both sides of the Atlantic and that through various literary publications.

Dutton had been writing for a number of years before her second husband's demise. After his death a steady stream of tracts and treatises, collections of selected correspondence, and poems poured forth from her pen. Among her numerous correspondents were a number of key figures in the eighteenth-century Evangelical Revival: the Welsh preacher Howel Harris (1714–1773), the redoubtable Selina Hastings, the Countess of Huntingdon (1707–

---

[18] Cited Sciretti, "Feed My Lambs," 91–92.
[19] Ivimey, *History of the English Baptists*, 4:510.

1791), and George Whitefield.[20] Harris was convinced that the Lord had entrusted her "with a talent of writing for him."[21] When William Seward (1711-1740), an early Methodist preacher who was killed by a mob in Wales, read a letter she had written to him in May, 1739, he found it "full of such comforts and direct answers to what I had been writing that it filled my eyes with tears of joy."[22] And Whitefield, who helped promote and publish Dutton's writings, once said after a meeting with her: "her conversation is as weighty as her letters."[23]

By 1740 she had written seven books. Another fourteen followed between 1741 and 1743, and fourteen more by 1750.[24] And there were yet more, for she continued to write up until her death in 1765. She was clearly the most prolific female Baptist author of the eighteenth century. But she wrestled with whether it was biblical for her to be an authoress. In a tract entitled *A Letter To such of the Servants of Christ, who May have any Scruples about the Lawfulness of Printing any Thing written by a Woman* (1743), she maintained that she wrote not for fame, but for "only the glory of God, and the good of souls."[25] To those who might accuse of her violating 1 Timothy 2:12, she answered that her books were not intended to be read in a public setting of worship, which the 1 Timothy text was designed to address. Rather, the instruction that her books gave was private, for they were read by believers in "their

---

[20] See the discussion of these links by Stein, "A Note on Anne Dutton," 485-490, and Sciretti, "Feed My Lambs," 198-280.

[21] Cited Stein, "A Note on Anne Dutton," 487-488.

[22] Cited Stein, "A Note on Anne Dutton," 488.

[23] George Whitefield, Letter to Mr. [Jonathan] B[ryan], July 24, 1741 in *Letters of George Whitefield For the period 1734-1742* (1771 ed.; repr. Edinburgh: The Banner of Truth Trust, 1976), 280.

[24] Sciretti, "Feed My Lambs," 100-101.

[25] Anne Dutton, *A Letter To such of the Servants of Christ, who May have any Scruples about the Lawfulness of Printing any Thing written by a Woman* in Watson, comp., *Selected Spiritual Writings of Anne Dutton*, 3:254.

own private houses."²⁶ She asked those who opposed women writers to "Imagine then ... when my books come to your house, that I am come to give you a visit" and to "patiently attend" to her infant "lispings."²⁷ What if some other authoresses had used the press for "trifles"? Well, she answered, "shall none of that sex be suffer'd to appear on Christ's side, to tell of the wonders of his love, to seek the good of souls, and the advancement of the Redeemer's interest?"²⁸

Talking/Writing about the Trinity
Dutton was not slow to critique theological positions she felt erroneous or inadequate. In 1757, for example, she happened to read William Romaine's *A Discourse upon the Self-Existence of Jesus Christ* (1755). Romaine, at the time the only Evangelical Anglican clergyman in the English capital,²⁹ had preached this sermon on John 8:24 ("I said therefore unto you, that ye shall die in your sins: for if ye believe not, that I am, ye shall die in your sins") two years earlier and had it published the same year. In the published version Romaine gave a powerful defence of the essential deity of Jesus Christ—and thus a rebuttal of two major heresies of the eighteenth century, Socinianism and Deism—and was also insistent that the "doctrine of the Trinity is the most necessary article of the Christian religion."³⁰ It went through at least five editions in

---

[26] Dutton, *Printing any Thing written by a Woman* in Watson, comp., *Selected Spiritual Writings of Anne Dutton*, 3:254.
[27] Dutton, *Printing any Thing written by a Woman* in Watson, comp., *Selected Spiritual Writings of Anne Dutton*, 3:257.
[28] Dutton, *Printing any Thing written by a Woman* in Watson, comp., *Selected Spiritual Writings of Anne Dutton*, 3:256.
[29] On Romaine, see especially Tim Shenton, *'An Iron Pillar': The Life and Times of William Romaine* (Darlington, England/Webster, NY: Evangelical Press, 2004). See also the classic account of Romaine's life and ministry by J.C. Ryle, *The Christian Leaders of the Last Century; or, England a Hundred Years Ago* (London: T. Nelson and Sons, 1880), 149-179.
[30] William Romaine, *A Discourse upon the Self-Existence of Jesus Christ* (4th ed.; London: J. Worrall and E. Withers, 1756), 19. For the historical context of the sermon, see

the 1750s and was still being reprinted as late as 1788 (the seventh edition).

In one portion of the sermon, though, Dutton believed that Romaine's language smacked of Sabellianism, or modalism. Romaine was replying to critics of the nomenclature used to describe the persons of the Godhead, namely, Father, Son, and Holy Spirit:

> They suppose, with ignorance common to infidelity, that these names were to give us ideas of the manner, in which the persons exist in the essence [of God], but the Scripture had quite a different view in using them. The ever blessed Trinity took the names of Father, Son, and Holy Spirit, not to describe in what manner they exist as divine persons, but in what manner the divine persons have acted for us, and for our salvation. These names were to give us ideas of the distinct offices, which the Trinity had agreed to sustain in the œconomy of our redemption. The Scripture informs us ... that the covenant of grace was made before the world, and the gracious plan of man's salvation was settled before he had his being. According to the plan of this covenant one of the divine persons agreed to demand infinite satisfaction for sin, when mankind should offend, and to be the Father of the human nature of Jesus Christ, and our Father through him; and therefore he is called God the Father, not to describe his nature, but his office. Another of the divine persons covenanted to become a son, to take our nature upon him, and in it to pay the infinite satisfaction for sin, and therefore he is called Son, Son of God, and such like names, not to describe his divine nature, but his divine office. Another of the divine persons covenanted to make the infinite satisfaction of the Son of God effectual, by inspiring the spirits of men, and disposing them to receive it, and therefore he is called the holy Inspirer, or Holy Spirit, and the

---

Shenton, *'An Iron Pillar'*, 127–129. I first read this sermon by Romaine in November of 2003, and felt then that Romaine did not clearly distinguish his conception of the Godhead from modalism.

> Spirit of God, not to describe his divine nature but his divine office. The terms Father, Son, and Holy Spirit, are terms of œconomy and are accordingly used in Scripture, to describe the distinct parts, which the ever blessed and adorable Trinity sustained in our redemption.
>
> ... The Scripture makes no difference between the divine persons, except what is made by the distinct offices, which they sustain in the covenant of grace. The persons are equal in every perfection and attribute; none is before or after other; none is greater or less than another; but the whole three persons are co-eternal together and co-equal. And consequently Christ, who was from eternity co-equal with the Father, did not make himself inferior, because he covenanted to become a Son, nor did the Holy Spirit, who was from eternity co-equal with the Father and the Son, make himself inferior, because he covenanted to make the spirits of men holy by his grace and influence. Son and Holy Spirit are names of office, and the names of their offices certainly cannot lessen the dignity of their nature, but should rather exalt them in our eyes, for whose salvation they condescended to sustain these offices.[31]

This text more than adequately displays Romaine's commitment to the affirmation that there are three persons within the Godhead and that these three persons are absolutely co-equal and co-eternal. But it is noteworthy that Romaine does not attempt to distinguish the divine persons by classical patristic terms, namely, the Father's ingenerateness, the Son's eternal generation and the Holy Spirit's eternal procession. In fact, he appears to argue against this way of distinguishing the divine persons. The divine persons are to be differentiated on the basis of the roles that they play in the economy of salvation. The term "Son," for example, says nothing about his divine nature, but about the office he bore to effect the salvation of sinners. Likewise, the name "Holy

---

[31] Romaine, *Discourse upon the Self-Existence of Jesus Christ*, 18–20.

Spirit" says nothing about his relationship to the other two persons of the Godhead, but has to do with the way he persuades sinners to believe in Christ.

When Dutton read Romaine's sermon, she was "loth to think" that Romaine was not truly Trinitarian, but she was convinced that he had "given great countenance to the Sabellian error." The above-cited text essentially distinguished the divine persons solely on the basis of their work in salvation.[32] Dutton thus asked whether or not "the three divine persons ... were not Father, Son, and Spirit, prior to their agreeing to act" in eternity past for the salvation of fallen humanity?[33]

She then indicated how she would distinguish the persons by means of classical Nicene Trinitarian terminology:

> [T]hose proper names, by which these divine persons are described in the Holy Scriptures, are doubtless descriptive, if not of their nature, as God; yet of their distinct subsistences in, and as possessing of the divine essence, with their mutual relations to each other therein. So that the first divine person, with respect to his begetting the second divine person, is called the Father, and to beget his Son, is the peculiar property of God the Father. The second divine person, with respect to his ineffable and eternal generation, in the divine essence, is called the Son; and to be the only-begotten of the Father, is the peculiar property of God the Son. And the third divine person with respect to his proceeding from the Father and the Son, in the divine essence, is called the Spirit; and to proceed from both, as the Spirit of the Father and the Son, is the peculiar property of God the Spirit. And tho' there is no priority, nor posteriority, among these divine persons: so that one was before, and another after the other, and a third after both, with regard to the order of time; but each of these three divine

---

[32] Dutton, *Divine Eternal Sonship of Jesus Christ*, 4–5.
[33] Dutton, *Divine Eternal Sonship of Jesus Christ*, 6.

> subsistences, did together and at once necessarily exist in the eternal self-existent essence of Jehovah. Yet I humbly think, that we may, yea, must conceive, according to the Scripture-names given to these divine persons, with their relative properties, that there was priority, and posteriority, with respect to the order of nature. And yet this infers not any superiority, nor inferiority, among the divine persons: in that the three distinct subsistences, do jointly possess, all the immense and eternal glories, of the one undivided, infinite essence of Jehovah... in which these three divine persons are co-equal, co-essential, and co-eternal.[34]

Like Romaine, Dutton affirmed her conviction that the three divine persons are "co-equal, co-essential, and co-eternal." The three are "undivided" and share to the full the "infinite essence" of deity. Unlike Romaine, however, Dutton was not chary about using the patristic language of generation and procession to distinguish the three persons. The different names used in the Bible of the three persons speak of eternal relationships in which there is no sense of lesser or greater, but which nonetheless speaks of an order: only the Father could beget the Son, only the Son could be begotten, and only the Spirit could proceed from both the Father and the Son. *Pace* the implications of Romaine's explanation of the divine names, these relationships are not arbitrary. As Dutton sums up her position:

> ... the Son's being begotten of the Father, and the Spirit's proceeding from both, makes no superiority, nor inferiority, among the divine persons, as each possess the same infinite essence; but only denotes the particular manner and order, in which the divine essence necessarily exists.[35]

---

[34] Dutton, *Divine Eternal Sonship of Jesus Christ*, 6-7, 8.
[35] Dutton, *Divine Eternal Sonship of Jesus Christ*, 14.

To Dutton's way of thinking, to deny that the divine names describe the "distinct subsistences in the divine essence" is "nothing less than to rob them of their personality; and so, of their divine glory."[36]

Two Other Baptist Critiques

It is noteworthy that Dutton's younger Baptist contemporary, Benjamin Beddome (1717–1795), the pastor of the Particular Baptist cause in Bourton-on-the-Water, was also familiar with this idiosyncrasy of Romaine's Trinitarian theology. In a sermon on Mark 12:28–31 that Romaine published in 1760, the Anglican minister had stated:

> The right knowledge of God then consists in believing, that in Jehovah the self-existence essence there are three co-equal and co-eternal persons, between whom there is no difference or inequality, but what is made by the covenant of grace. Their names Father, Son, and Holy Spirit, are not descriptive of their nature, but of their offices, they are not to teach us in what manner they exist in Jehovah, but they are covenant names, belonging to the offices, which the divine persons sustain in the covenant. The scripture does not use these names to teach us, how the divine persons exist, but how they act; how they stand related to the heirs of promise, and not what they are in themselves, as persons in Jehovah. This is a truth of great importance, which I have endeavoured to defend both from the pulpit and from the press, and particularly in a printed discourse upon the self-existence of Jesus Christ. The true object of worship then, to whom our obedience and love are due, is Jehovah Alehim,[37]

---

[36] Dutton, *Divine Eternal Sonship of Jesus Christ*, 8.

[37] "Alehim" here would appear to be Romaine's term for what is now transliterated as "Elohim."

according to what is said in the Creed, "the unity in Trinity and the Trinity in unity is to be worshipped."[38]

In an undated sermon entitled *Christ manifested to the soul*,[39] Beddome cited this very passage and then noted that "others contend"—was he aware of Dutton's critique of Romaine?—that the term "Son" is

> a title belonging to Christ as the second Person in the ever-blessed Trinity, and expressive of both of equality of essence, and the peculiar relation in which he stands to the Divine Father; and that this is an article of faith which enters into the experience and worship of God's people.[40]

Beddome himself was of the opinion that the term "Son" could "be understood in both these senses" in "different passages of Scripture."[41]

The doyen of Baptist theology in this era, John Gill,[42] was also quite critical of the sort of Trinitarian reflection proposed by Romaine. He did not mention him by name, but it is unlikely he was not acquainted with his views as both men ministered in the English capital during the 1750s and 1760s. In fact, on one occasion during the early to mid-1750s, Gill had breakfast with Romaine, along with Gill's friend James Hervey (1714-1758), George Whitefield, and John Wesley (1703-1791).[43] For Gill, the eternal

---

[38] William Romaine, "Upon the right Love of the Lord God" in his *Twelve Discourses upon the Law and the Gospel. Preached at St. Dunstan's Church in the West, London* (London: J. Worrall and M. Withers, 1760), 262-263.

[39] In Benjamin Beddome, *Sermons Printed from the Manuscripts of the Late Rev. Benjamin Beddome, A.M.* (London: William Ball, 1835), 119-127. I owe this reference to my doctoral student, Rev. Daniel Ramsey of Cleveland, Ohio.

[40] *Sermons Printed from the Manuscripts of the Late Rev. Benjamin Beddome*, 119.

[41] *Sermons Printed from the Manuscripts of the Late Rev. Benjamin Beddome*, 119.

[42] For Gill, see above, Chapter 4.

[43] Aaron C. H. Seymour, *The Life and Times of Selina Countess of Huntingdon* (London: William Edward Painter, 1840), 1:162.

Sonship of Christ, and thus his eternal generation, "is an article of the greatest importance in the Christian religion," even its "distinguishing criterion," without which "the doctrine of the Trinity can never be supported."[44] As Gill argued in his systematic theology, published in 1769, without eternal Sonship (and the eternal spiration of the Spirit), there is nothing to distinguish the different persons within the Godhead in eternity past:

> Those men I have now respect to, hold that there are three distinct persons in the Godhead, or divine nature; and therefore it must be something in the divine nature, and not any thing out of it, that distinguishes them; not any works *ad extra*, done by them; nor their concern in the economy of man's salvation; nor office bore by them, which are arbitrary things, which might, or might not have been, had it pleased God.[45]

Gill especially took aim at the thinking of the Congregationalist Thomas Ridgley (1667–1734), who maintained a position identical to that of Romaine: Sonship has to do with the office of mediator, not the internal relationship of the first and second persons of the Godhead.[46] As Gill responded to Ridgley—and he would have said the same to Romaine: without the Son's eternal generation "no proof can be made of his being a distinct divine person in the Godhead."[47]

---

[44] John Gill, *A Complete Body of Doctrinal and Practical Divinity* (New ed.; London: W. Winterbotham, 1796), 1:209, 210.

[45] Gill, *Body of Doctrinal and Practical Divinity*, 1:205, 207.

[46] See Gill, *Body of Doctrinal and Practical Divinity*, 1:210–212. For the text that Gill is criticizing, see Thomas Ridgley, *A Body of Divinity* (London: Daniel Midwinter, Aaron Ward, John Oswald; and Richard Hett, 1731), 121-131.

[47] Gill, *Body of Doctrinal and Practical Divinity*, 1:210.

Coda

There were at least three reprints of Romaine's *A Discourse upon the Self-Existence of Jesus Christ* after Dutton's robust critique, but his argument remained unaltered. It is possible he was unaware of her letter, but her friendship with fellow Evangelicals like Whitefield, who also knew Romaine well, makes this unlikely.[48] Did the Anglican preacher believe then that Dutton's criticism was not worth answering? If so, he would have been very mistaken. Dutton was indeed right to critique his failure to use classic terminology to differentiate the three within the Godhead. In his sermon, Romaine had rightly asserted: "The doctrine of the Trinity is the most necessary article of the Christian religion, and we cannot take one step in the way to heaven, without being clear in it."[49] Dutton's letter provided a clarity that Romaine's sermon—and one might add, current quarters of Evangelicalism—greatly needed.

---

[48] For Romaine's friendship with Whitefield, see Shenton, *'An Iron Pillar'*, 167–169.

[49] Romaine, *Discourse upon the Self-Existence of Jesus Christ*, 19.

6
"Not the same God": Alexander Carson and the Ulster Trinitarian Controversy

Ian Hugh Clary

The Protestant Reformation and its heirs in the post-Reformation period put a premium on confessional subscription. From the early Reformed symbols such as the Belgic Confession to the Westminster Standards of a few generations later, Protestants of various stripes took their denominational confessions seriously as part of their ecclesial and national identities.[1] While there were notable differences between Protestant confessions, often for geographical and national reasons, there was a fundamental core that they shared with each other and with the catholic tradition stretching back to the theology of the ecumenical creeds. This unifying, biblical, and tradition-oriented confessionalism changed dramatically in the long eighteenth century when a decided move away from confessional orthodoxy occurred at the infamous Salters' Hall Synod of 1719. There, a group of Dissenting leaders representing the Presbyterian, Independent, and Baptist denominations decided by a close-margin vote that confessional

---

[1] Carl R. Trueman makes the point that confessionalism was related to the fragmentation of society after the Reformation, where both denominations and nations sought to carve out their particular identities. See Carl R. Trueman, *The Creedal Imperative* (Wheaton, IL: Crossway, 2012), 109. For more modern debates on confessional subscription see J. V. Fesko, *The Need for Creeds Today: Confessional Faith in a Faithless Age* (Grand Rapids, MI: Baker Academic, 2020). For historical takes on confessional subscription in the Reformed tradition see the essays by Peter Lillback and W. Robert Godfrey in David W. Hall, ed., *The Practice of Confessional Subscription* (Powder Springs, GA: Covenant Foundation, 2018).

subscription was not a requirement for ordination in their respective churches. This resulted in the waxing and waning of confessionalism within British Nonconformity that had a deleterious impact on catholic doctrines like the deity of Christ, the nature of the atonement, and relevant to this essay, the doctrine of the Trinity.[2]

The ensuing debate over such doctrines in relation to confessional subscription has been traced in a number of important works on British Nonconformity, particularly those of Philip Dixon and Paul C. H. Lim.[3] Yet little focus has been given to how those debates played out in a northern Irish context. This chapter will trace the debate over confessional subscription and its impact on the doctrine of the Trinity in Irish Dissent illustrating it with a particular, though brief, summary of aspects of an Irish conflict between the Baptist Alexander Carson and the Unitarian William Hamilton Drummond. It will begin by looking at the larger question of subscription in England and Ireland and how it would impact the Ulster Synod. Then it will turn specifically to the debate over the Trinity between Carson and Drummond, though due to space constraints, we will focus on two aspects of that debate, one theological and the other philosophical, to get some sense of how it played out in the Ireland of the long eighteenth century. Thus we can trace the impact of the Salter's Hall Synod on the Ulster Synod and what effect it had for a key orthodox doctrine.

---

[2] An excellent study of non-subscription in Britain and Ireland is Charles Scott Sealy, "Church Authority and Non-Subscription Controversies in Early 18th Century Presbyterianism" (PhD dissertation, University of Glasgow, 2010).

[3] Philip Dixon, *"Nice and Hot Disputes": The Doctrine of the Trinity in the Seventeenth Century* (London: T&T Clark, 2003); Paul C. H. Lim, *Mystery Unveiled: The Crisis of the Trinity in Early Modern England*, Oxford Studies in Historical Theology (Oxford: Oxford University Press, 2012). It is important to note that Lim's work deals primarily with the seventeenth century.

Ian Hugh Clary

Subscription and Unitarianism in British Nonconformity

The Salters' Hall Synod was related in some measure to the growth of Unitarianism in the British Isles whose origins can be traced back at least to the Socinianism of the seventeenth century, particularly the influence of John Biddle (1616-1662) and his translation of the Racovian Catechism.[4] By the eighteenth century, a number within Dissenting leadership denied the deity of Christ, upholding a Unitarian view tantamount to Arianism. Others, though maintaining Trinitarian orthodoxy, nevertheless did not think that Trinitarian belief was necessary for ministerial ordination in Dissenting churches. British Unitarianism was influenced by the work of deists like Samuel Clarke (1675-1729) and Joseph Priestley (1733-1804) who also argued against using religious tests beyond the bible which they deemed the only "rule of faith."[5] In terms of legislation, non-subscription and related Unitarianism was made possible as far back as the Act of Toleration (1689) that required subscription to the Thirty-Nine Articles, but allowed for exceptions to be taken on matters pertaining to ceremonies, traditions, and homilies. Even more so, the Heads of Agreement (1691) loosened subscription further such that the bible was described as *the* rule of faith to be subscribed to, and only those parts of the Articles or the Westminster Confession that

---

[4] For Biddle and orthodox responses to him see Lim, *Mystery Unveiled*, 16-68, 124-171. Two other important studies on Socinianism and Unitarianism in England are H. John McLachlan, *Socinianism in Seventeenth-Century England* (London: Oxford University Press, 1951) and Sarah Mortimer, *Reason and Religion in the English Revolution: The Challenge of Socinianism* (Cambridge: Cambridge University Press, 2010). For a summary of Biddle's theology as it engaged with British Reformed Orthodoxy see Kelly M. Kapic, "The Spirit as Gift: Explorations in John Owen's Pneumatology," Kelly M. Kapic and Mark Jones, eds., *The Ashgate Research Companion to John Owen's Theology* (Surrey, UK: Ashgate Publishing, 2015), 117-118.

[5] Andrew Thompson, *The Oxford History of Protestant Dissenting Traditions: The Long Eighteenth Century c. 1689-c. 1828* (Oxford: Oxford University Press, 2018), 3:23. Clarke was an Arian and famously argued against the Trinity in his influential book *The Scripture-Doctrine of the Trinity* (1712). See Thomas C. Pfizenmaier, *The Trinitarian Theology of Dr. Samuel Clarke (1675-1729): Context, Sources, and Controversy* (Leiden: Brill, 1997).

were deemed "doctrinal."⁶ The eighteenth-century subscription controversies pushed this loosening even further.

For instance, over time, parts of British Dissent adopted certain requirements for ordination but not all of them required confessional subscription. This was seen explicitly in the Durham town of Crook where Samuel Bourn the Younger (1689-1754) refused to subscribe to the Westminster Standards at his 1711 ordination. Likewise, John Taylor (1694-1761), an Arian, did not subscribe to any confession at his Presbyterian ordination in Derbyshire in 1716.⁷ The issue of non-subscription came to a head when Martin Tompkins (died ca. 1755) preached at Stoke Newington, Middlesex, and openly criticised the doctrine of the Trinity, resulting in his expulsion from the congregation in 1718. Tompkins had argued against the imposition of the creeds and his view was taken up in Exeter by James Peirce (ca. 1674-1726), who argued likewise in 1717. Peirce, it is worth noting, was an acquaintance of William Whiston (1667-1752), an Arian at Cambridge. Hubert Stogdon (1692-1728), who had been trained at Exeter Academy, was ordained using his own personal creed. In a letter written in 1718 speaking against

> the tyrannical fetters of blind obedience and implicit faith from men's minds apace ... Men will no longer take things on trust; nor believe them because our forefathers, though ever so pious and venerable, told them so or so. But they will now immediately to the law and testimony; search the scriptures themselves and see whether it be so or no.⁸

---

⁶ Thompson, *Oxford History*, 3:23.

⁷ Taylor forcefully argued against the classical doctrine of the imputation of Adam's sin in his *The Scripture Doctrine of Original Sin* (1740). See Alan P. F. Sell, David J. Hall, and Ian Sellers, eds., *Protestant Nonconformist Texts 2: The Eighteenth Century* (Eugene, OR: Wipf and Stock, 2015), 48.

⁸ Cited in James C. Spalding, "The Demise of English Presbyterianism: 1660-1760," *Church History* 28.1 (March 1959): 76.

Ian Hugh Clary

The so-called Exeter Controversy was to be adjudicated by Dissenting ministers in London who met at Salters' Hall on February, 24, 1719; their primary intention was to deal with the matter of confessional subscription, though Unitarianism was closely related. It was decided by a vote of 57 to 53 that confessional subscription was not required for ordination, nor did ordinands necessarily have to adhere to belief in the Trinity. It should be noted that only a few of those who voted against subscription were openly Arian, nevertheless, the Synod's results split churches and denominations across the British Isles.[9]

John Abernethey, Non-subscription and Arianism in Ulster
The general effects of the non-subscription movement and Arianism were felt beyond just London and Exeter but went north into Scotland and across the Irish Sea into Ireland.[10] The notable example in Scotland is John Simson (ca. 1668–1740), Professor of Divinity at the University of Glasgow, who underwent trial before Church of Scotland courts for Arianism and was eventually suspended from his faculty duties.[11] In Dublin the Presbyterian minister Thomas Emlyn (1663–1741) was imprisoned and fined due to his Unitarian work, *Humble Inquiry into the Scripture Account of Jesus Christ* (1702). In Belfast John Abernethey (1680–1740) "shook

---

[9] Thompson, *Oxford History*, 3:24.

[10] James Moore notes the role that the philosopher Francis Hutcheson (1694–1746) played in his emphasis on the right to private judgment on the issue of subscription in both Scotland and Ireland. Hutcheson's concerns were philosophically grounded in the right to free thought in relation to ecclesiastical authority. James Moore, "Presbyterianism and the Right of Private Judgment: Church Government in Ireland and Scotland in the Age of Francis Hutcheson," in Ruth Savage, ed., *Philosophy & Religion in Enlightenment Britain* (Oxford: Oxford University Press, 2012), 141–168.

[11] For Simson see Anne Skoczylas, *Mr. Simson's Knotty Case: Divinity, Politics, and Due Process in Early Eighteenth-Century Scotland* (Montreal and Kingston: McGill-Queen's University Press, 2001).

the orthodoxy of Presbyterianism in the north of Ireland" due to his non-subscription views.[12]

Abernethy's story provides important context for the figures under review in this essay as he was deemed a contributing factor to the rise of Arianism within the Synod of Ulster in the long eighteenth century, though not himself an Arian. He had been trained at Edinburgh University under the Professor of Divinity, George Campbell (d. 1701), a convert to episcopacy and who was responsible for the training of many Irish Presbyterians.[13] Abernethy was licensed to preach in 1702 in the Presbytery of Antrim where he was installed as a minister after having declined an invitation to take over for Emlyn in Dublin.[14] Abernethy was, with James Kirkpatrick (ca. 1676-1743), instrumental in founding the Belfast Society that brought ministers, licentiates, and lay-people together to discuss theology, sermons, and books, but also had the express purpose of bringing "things to the test of reason and scripture without servile regard to any human authority."[15] One such human authority was the Westminster Confession of Faith (1644) to which subscription was required by all Ulster Presbyterian ministers. On December 19, 1719, Abernethy preached before the Society a sermon entitled "Religious Obedience Founded on Personal Persuasion," and argued that submission was only to be to Christ's teaching and not any "human declarations and decisions in any point of faith or duty." Persons were to follow "impartially

---

[12] Richard B. Barlow, "The Career of John Abernethy (1680-1740) Father of Non-subscription in Ireland and Defender of Religious Liberty," *Harvard Theological Review* 78:3-4 (July-October 1985), 400.

[13] For Campbell as episcopalian see Ryan K. Frace, "Religious Toleration in the Wake of Revolution: Scotland on the Eve of Enlightenment (1688-1710s)," *History* 93.311 (July 2008), 361.

[14] Barlow, "Career of John Abernethy," 401.

[15] "Abernethy (John)," *The Encyclopedia of Religious Knowledge*, ed. J. Newton Brown (Brattleboro, VT: Joseph Steen & Co., 1846), 14. See also Robert Whan, *The Presbyterians of Ulster, 1680-1730* (Woodbridge, UK: The Boydell Press, 2013), 11-13.

their own light."[16] This sparked intense controversy amongst Ulster Presbyterians with camps divided over whether to subscribe to the Westminster Standards or not; those of Abernethy's persuasion were deemed "New Light" and Arminian.[17] In 1720 the controversy was addressed by the General Synod of Ulster with the "Pacific Act" that maintained confessional subscription, but allowed ordinands to take exceptions, wherein they could substitute their own preferred language about an excepted doctrine, so long as it adhered to the general principles of the faith.[18]

The Westminster Confession stood staunchly in the catholic tradition in its affirmation of the doctrine of the Trinity. Article 2 of the Confession states that there is "but one only living and true God" (2.1) who "is alone in and unto himself allsufficient ... [and] is the alone foundation of being" (2.2) and yet "in the unity of the Godhead there be three persons, of one substance, power, and eternity: God the Father, God the Son, and God the Holy Ghost" (2.3).[19] With this confession of faith pushed to the side in terms of subscription, it was much easier for those who denied the doctrine of the Trinity as laid out in these articles to gain ordination in the Irish Presbyterian churches. Abernethy argued that his non-subscriptionism was not because he disagreed with the Confession on points of doctrine, but that he valued the dignity of freedom of conscience for those who did. In the midst of this controversy, another erupted over Thomas Nevin (ca. 1686–1744),

---

[16] John Abernethy, "Religious Obedience Founded on Personal Persuasion," in *Scarce and Valuable Tracts and Sermons occasionally Published by the late Reverend and Learned John Abernethy, MA*. (London, 1751), 252-253. Cited in Barlow, "Career of John Abernethy," 405.

[17] David Steers, "Arminianism amongst Protestant Dissenters in England and Ireland in the Eighteenth Century," in Th. Marius van Leeuwen, Keith D. Stranglin, Marijke Tolsma, eds., *Arminius, Arminianism, and Europe: Jacobus Arminius (1559/60-1609)*, Brill's Series in Church History (Leiden: Brill, 2009), 172.

[18] Barlow, "Career of John Abernethy," 406.

[19] "The Westminster Confession of Faith, 1646," in R. Tudor Jones, Arthur Long, and Rosemary Moore, eds., *Protestant Nonconformist Texts 1: 1550-1700* (Aldershot, UK: Ashgate, 2007), 167-168.

minister in Downpatrick, who argued that it was not blasphemous to deny the deity of Christ. He was brought to trial before the synod in 1724 and when he refused to recant his belief he was removed from the synod's membership, though he maintained his pastoral charge.[20] The upset caused by this dispute was muted by the over-arching controversy over subscription, eventuating in the synod's pragmatic decision to move all non-subscribers into the Presbytery of Antrim. Though still under the jurisdiction of the Ulster Synod, the Antrim Presbytery was effectively free to allow Unitarians within its ministerial fold, which it did. Though the Ulster Synod never formally allowed for Unitarianism, the influence of Antrim was significant. Arianism would soon surpass the controversy over subscription in the Ulster Synod, and would not finally be put down by the orthodox until the leadership of Henry Cooke (1788–1868).[21]

Interlocutors: Drummond and Carson

The controversy over Arianism within Irish Presbyterianism can be seen in microcosm in the debate between the Unitarian William Hamilton Drummond and the Presbyterian-turned-Baptist Alexander Carson who engaged in a written controversy over the Trinity that originated in and went beyond the bounds of Irish Presbyterianism. Both controversialists knew each other from their student days in Glasgow, both had served Presbyterian churches in the North, though Drummond as part of the Presbytery of Antrim and Carson of Tyrone. Drummond's writings on issues pertaining to Unitarianism prompted an irenic but forceful reply from Carson. Before considering this exchange, a brief biographical sketch of each will help further set the context.

---

[20] Barlow, "Career of John Abernethy," 408.
[21] Henry Leebody, "Henry Cooke, D.D., and Arianism in the Irish Church," *The Presbyterian Quarterly and Princeton Review* 1/2 (April 1872): 205–231.

Ian Hugh Clary

Alternative Ulster: William Hamilton Drummond (1778-1865)
Drummond was born in Larne, Co. Antrim, in August 1778, though was raised in Belfast after the passing of his father.[22] He was educated at the Belfast Academy and spent some time in England with the hopes of going into manufacturing. He soon left England for Glasgow where he studied at Glasgow College (part of the University of Glasgow) in 1794, though he did not obtain his degree due to financial stresses. It was common for Ulster Presbyterians to send their ministers-in-training to Glasgow to be educated, wherein they received an education that was "a mixture of orthodoxy and Enlightenment."[23] Though he left before graduation, Drummond obtained an interest in classical learning and began to write poetry. In terms of classics, he produced a translation of the Epicurean philosopher Lucretius' (ca. 94-95) famous poem *Of the Nature of Things*.[24] He also wrote a number of noteworthy poems and hymns himself; one famous elegy eulogized that nation-defining event at Trafalgar and another poem described Northern Ireland's great expression of natural beauty in the Giant's Causeway.[25] In the latter he addressed himself to the "Genius of my natal shore."[26] After Glasgow Drummond returned to Ulster and trained in the Armagh Presbytery which, like Antrim, did not require confessional subscription. He was licensed to preach in 1800 in Belfast, under the authority of the Antrim Presbytery. Drummond was a literary figure as well as a minister, and was a key founding member of the Belfast Literary Society (1801).

---

[22] For more, see the entry on Drummond in the *Oxford Dictionary of National Biography* 16:995-996.

[23] Andrew R. Holmes, *The Shaping of Ulster Presbyterian Belief and Practice, 1770-1840* (Oxford: Oxford University Press, 2006), 136.

[24] Lucretius, *First Book of T. Lucretius Carus, Of the Nature of Things*, trans. William Hamilton Drummond (Edinburgh: Mundell, Doig, and Stevenson, 1808).

[25] William Hamilton Drummond, *The Battle of Trafalgar, A Heroic Poem* (Belfast: J. Smyth and D. Lyons, 1806); idem., *The Giants' Causeway, a Poem* (Belfast: Joseph Smyth, 1811).

[26] Drummond, *Giant's Causeway*, 3.

He was also an early advocate of animal rights, arguing in a short tract published in 1830 that such rights were grounded in human obligation before God to care for nature.[27] Not only did Drummond pastor in Belfast, but also in Dublin for a time. His academic ability was recognised by his admission into the Royal Irish Academy due to his theological works such as the one on the Trinity under review in this chapter. Perhaps his most notorious work was his biography of Michael Servetus (d. 1553), the famed sixteenth-century Unitarian who was executed in Calvin's Geneva—Drummond described Servetus in the sub-title of his work as committing the "alleged crime of heresy" wherein he was "entrapped, imprisoned, and burned by John Calvin the Reformer."[28] He also obtained a D.D. degree from Aberdeen University at the behest of Bishop Percy of Dromore. He died in Dublin in October 1865.

Ulster Boy: Alexander Carson (1776–1844)

Drummond's great critic on the doctrine of the Trinity was his fellow Ulsterman Alexander Carson who had also served as a minister in the Presbyterian Church, though eventually he would leave the Ulster Synod over differing ecclesiological convictions. Carson was born in Annahone, Co. Tyrone, to Scots-Irish parents.[29] They raised him in the Presbyterian church wherein he learned the Westminster Confession of Faith and from a young age he showed an aptitude for learning. After receiving a classical education in Tullyhogue, which served also as pre-ministerial training, he matriculated at the University of Glasgow where for a

---

[27] William Hamilton Drummond, *Humanity to Animals, The Christian's Duty; A Discourse* (Cork: King and Ridings, 1830).

[28] William Hamilton Drummond, *The Life of Michael Servetus: The Spanish Physician, Who, for the Alleged Crime of Heresy, Was Entrapped, Imprisoned, and Burned By John Calvin the Reformer, in the City of Geneva, October 27, 1553* (London: John Chapman, 1848).

[29] For more on Carson's life see Ian Hugh Clary, "Alexander Carson (1776–1844): 'Jonathan Edwards of the Nineteenth Century," *American Theological Inquiry* 2.2 (2009): 43–52.

time he was a fellow student of Drummond's. There he excelled in studies of philosophy, ethics, Hebrew, Greek, Latin, logic, and theology. In particular, he studied Greek under John Young (ca. 1747–1820), a noted philologist. At Glasgow Carson obtained BA and MA degrees. Upon his return to Ireland he was ordained in the Tyrone Presbytery (1798), a pro-subscription presbytery, and then became the minister at the Presbyterian Church in Tobermore (sometimes Tubbermore).[30]

Carson would eventually recuse himself from the Synod of Ulster due to a change of ecclesiological convictions that he expressed in his *Reasons for Separating from the General Synod of Ulster* (1805). Though the problems over subscription were lurking in the background, his fundamental reason for leaving was over what he described as "promiscuous communion," or the administering of the Lord's Supper to those who were not regenerated Christians. The "decent worldling" could be found at the table, and however decent they may be morally, because they were of the world, they should not be admitted to the table.[31] What was required as a test of membership was their status in Christ, not whether they were merely moral in their character. This would lead him to develop Congregationalist convictions on church government.[32] Carson was, however, also quite concerned over the growing Arianism due to Antrim Presbytery's influence in the Synod. Unitarians and orthodox Christians did not worship the same God, according to Carson, and Antrim Presbytery's abiding

---

[30] See *Records of the General Synod of Ulster, From 1691–1820*, 3 vols. (Belfast: John Reid and Co., 1898), 3:217. The entry on Carson's ordination explicitly spells out his subscription to the Westminster Confession. I am indebted to John Gill, "The Evangelicalism of Alexander Carson" (unpublished PhD dissertation, The Southern Baptist Theological Seminary, 2012), 10, for this source.

[31] Alexander Carson, *Reasons for Separating from the General Synod of Ulster* (Belfast: Simms, 1805), 94.

[32] For Carson's changing ecclesiology see David Luke, "Alexander Carson (1776–1844) and the Case for Congregationalism," *Journal of European Baptist Studies* 17.2 (2017): 20–30.

influence was denigrating the theological integrity of Ulster Presbyterianism. As he said in *Reasons for Separating*, "A Calvinist and a Socinian or Arian, can with no propriety worship together. They do not address the same God."[33] Leaving Presbyterianism came at great cost in a place like Ulster. He described the effects of his leaving by saying, "The day I gave up my connexion with the general synod, I gave up all that the world esteems. I sacrifice not only my prospects in life, and my respectability in the world, but every settled way of support."[34]

Carson's views of church government continued to change after he engaged with Scottish Baptists influenced by Robert (1768-1851) and James Haldane (1764-1842), two influential Baptist leaders with whom Carson would develop a friendship.[35] These Baptists would convince Carson of believer's baptism which would eventuate in his founding of a Baptist church in Tobermore and the publication of the work he is best known for, *Baptism Its Mode and Subjects* (1844). Carson also worked closely with the Haldanes in their controversies over the doctrine of biblical inspiration, and it is said that Carson was a key source behind Robert Haldane's famous commentary on Romans.[36] Beyond his theological interests, Carson was in support of the growing missionary movement in Britain, and just before his death in 1844 had preached on behalf of the recently founded Baptist Missionary Society.

---

[33] Carson, *Reasons for Separating*, 116-117.

[34] Carson, *Reasons for Separating*, iv.

[35] A standard, though dated, study of the Haldane brothers is Alexander Haldane, *Lives of Robert and James Haldane* (1852; Edinburgh: Banner of Truth Trust, 1991). See also Deryck W. Lovegrove, "Unity and Separation: Contrasting Elements in the Thought and Practice of Robert and James Alexander Haldane" in Michael W. Casey and Douglas A. Foster, eds., *The Stone-Campbell Movement: An International Religious Tradition*. I owe this reference to Clint Humfrey of High River, Alberta.

[36] For Carson on the doctrine of scripture, see Ian Hugh Clary, "'Celebrate the Perfections of Our Common Standard': Alexander Carson (1776-1844) and the Supremacy of Scripture," *Journal of Baptist Studies* 6 (2014): 5-30.

Ian Hugh Clary

Drummond on the Trinity
Context: The Maguire/Pope Debate

The background to the debate between Drummond and Carson was another earlier one on the Trinity held in April 1827 between a Roman Catholic priest and Church of Ireland clergyman. Drummond's opening chapter of *The Doctrine of the Trinity* traces the basic elements of this particular debate with the purpose of expressing his disagreement with both disputants who, though of different ecclesial communions, were agreed upon the orthodoxy of the doctrine of the Trinity.[37] Thomas Maguire (1792–1847), the Roman Catholic, argued for the Trinity based upon the need for an infallible interpreter of scripture and tradition, namely the Roman Catholic magisterium. Richard T. P. Pope (1799–1859), on the other hand, argued for the Trinity against Socinianism based upon "a Scriptural foundation."[38] Interestingly, Drummond agreed with Maguire that the Trinity can only be established by tradition and the Roman magisterium, but agreed with Pope that both are inadequate as authorities for theological understanding. He disagreed with Maguire, however, that scripture or reason actually demonstrates the Trinity.

The Unitarian's Creed

What is most interesting, in light of the Unitarian unwillingness to subscribe to a confessional document, is that Drummond demonstrated the basic Unitarian position in the production of what he called, "The Unitarians' Creed." There is a sense of irony in this work inserted into his opening chapter because Drummond was adamantly opposed to the use of creeds or

---

[37] For a summary of the debate see *The Celebrated Controversial Discussion Between the Rev. Thomas Maguire and the Rev. Richard T. P. Pope, Which Took Place at the Lecture-Room of the Dublin Institution* (New York/Montreal: D. & J. Sadlier, 1874).

[38] William Hamilton Drummond, *The Doctrine of the Trinity, Founded Neither on Scripture, Nor on Reason and Common Sense, but on Tradition and the Infallible Church* (London: R. Hunter, 1831), 1.

confessions. His creed affirmed the radical oneness and simplicity of God who is "one in the strict and absolute sense of unity." He described God as "a spirit, simple, uncompounded, indivisible, without parallel or equal—self-existent—immutable—eternal—almighty—omiscient—omnipresent—possessed of wisdom, Truth, holiness, goodness, justice, with all other perfections, in their highest possible excellence."[39] This God, though just, does not possess "inextinguishable wrath" but instead an "infinite placability and mercy." Thus God requires "no bloody sacrifice," but rather, appealing to Psalm 51:17, the sacrifices of God are a broken and contrite heart. God is described also as the Father of all mankind, "whatever be their name, country, complexion, or creed." The Unitarians believed in the "revealed Word of God" in Old and New Testaments, and denied the use of creeds as "articles of human contrivance." The faith of the Unitarian is entirely expressed in "the very words of inspiration." The "pure light from heaven" requires, therefore, "no guidance from the dark lantern of tradition."[40] Later he will describe creeds as a "shackling of the mind," a damnatory imposition, and "devices of ecclesiastical tyranny."[41]

Regarding the "divinity of the Son of God," Drummond argued that in a sense his character, mission, doctrine, power, and authority were all "divine," but Christ himself was simply a moral teacher, exalted by God, but not himself God.[42] Of the Trinity itself, Drummond argued, the scriptures are silent. Thus, taking *sola scriptura* seriously (according to Drummond), to be Trinitarian is to be Roman Catholic, because it is only in the councils of the Roman Catholic Church that the Trinity is expressed. Here he looked to the early church and, aside from the Jerusalem

---

[39] Drummond, *Doctrine of the Trinity*, 2.
[40] Drummond, *Doctrine of the Trinity*, 3.
[41] Drummond, *Doctrine of the Trinity*, 5.
[42] Drummond, *Doctrine of the Trinity*, 3.

Council in Acts, all other councils were of no import. Church fathers were not to be looked to as authorities. Athanasius of Alexandria (d. 373) was described by Drummond as a "factious and turbulent ecclesiastic."[43] The idea of a Trinity of persons in the godhead went expressly against "reason and common sense" (hearkening to the subtitle of his book), which he believed were on the Unitarians' side.

Drummond's work is remarkable both for its depth and erudition. He did not take cheap swipes at Trinitarianism, but demonstrated a clear understanding of the arguments put forth by the orthodox of his day. Thus, his work goes into detailed discussions both of theology and scripture. Indeed, most of the work is devoted to key texts in Old and New Testaments typically appealed to as support for the Trinity. Theologically, he examined the names of Christ in the New Testament, arguing against their use as proofs for his deity. He gave attention to texts like 1 Timothy 3:16, 1 John 5:20, John 20:28, and the Carmen Christi of Philippians 2:5-11.[44] His argument over the latter likens the *morphe* that Christ shared with "God" with the *morphe* of the slave arguing that just as Christ came in the likeness of a slave, so he had the likeness of God, but was not God himself.[45] Much more could be said about his argumentation, but for the sake of time, we will examine his use of the terms "person" for the Trinity and his use of the philosophical categories of reason and common sense.

The second section of Drummond's opening chapter is called "What is Trinitarianism?" wherein he explained the theology that was handed down from Athanasius. Here he focused on the threeness of the persons, arguing against the Trinity based upon the word "person" itself. Quoting the Westminster Confession, he stated that the Trinity is best described as the view that says

---

[43] Drummond, *Doctrine of the Trinity*, 7.
[44] Drummond, *Doctrine of the Trinity*, 40-50.
[45] Drummond, *Doctrine of the Trinity*, 41-42.

that "the Godhead consists of 'three persons, of one substance, power, and eternity.'" These persons are "God the Father, God the Son, and God the Holy Ghost."[46] Here, the Confession makes use of the terminology of "person" as used in the early church. Drummond then addressed the definition of person using what he described as "reason and common sense," which should drive us to conclude "that three persons must mean three distinct beings." This in turn leads to polytheism, because the three persons turn out to be "three Gods."[47] Drummond appealed to a definition of "person" given by William Sherlock (ca. 1641-1707), Dean of St. Paul's Cathedral, in his *Vindication of the Doctrine of the Holy and Ever Blessed Trinity, and the Incarnation of the Son of God* (1690). Sherlock had said that a person "is an intelligent being, and to say there are three divine persons and not three distinct infinite minds, is both heresy and nonsense."[48] Drummond, following Sherlock's orthodox opponent Robert South (1634-1716), described this as "palpable polytheism."[49] To describe the three persons, as some did, as three modes of thinking that are grounded in one infinite mind merely explains away the problem by denying the personhood of the individual persons. If they are not persons,

---

[46] Drummond, *Doctrine of the Trinity*, 7.

[47] Drummond, *Doctrine of the Trinity*, 7, see also 108 and 120.

[48] William Sherlock, *A Vindication of the Doctrine of the Holy and Ever Blessed Trinity, and the Incarnation of the Son of God, Occasioned by the Brief Notes on the Creed of St. Athanasius, and the Brief History of the Unitarians, Or Socinians, and Containing an Answer to Both* (London: W. Rogers, 1690), 66. For a survey of Sherlock's Trinitarianism see Dixon, *"Nice and Hot Disputes,"* 109-114.

[49] Drummond, *Doctrine of the Trinity*, 7. Robert South was a Church of England minister and poet and strident episcopal antagonist during the Civil Wars. South wrote a critique of Sherlock's work on the Trinity arguing that it was effectively a form of tritheism. It is interesting to note that Drummond was willing to use the work of orthodox theologians if it served his Unitarian cause, though it would have been more helpful if he had actually engaged with the work of South instead of the novelties of Sherlock. See Robert South, *Tritheism charged upon Dr. Sherlock's new notion of the Trinity and the charge made good in an answer to the defense of the said notion against the Animadversions upon Dr. Sherlock's book, entituled, A vindication of the holy and ever-blessed Trinity* (London: John Whitlock, 1695). For South's critique of Sherlock's tritheism see Dixon, *"Nice and Hot Disputes,"* 123-125.

they must be something else, such as "three differences," per John Tillotson (1630–1694), or three "cogitations," according to the Saumur theologian Jean LeClerc (1657–1736); the latter Drummond argued was an expression of the rationalist philosophy of Renée Descartes (1596–1650).[50] With no person, there can be no union of persons in perichoresis. To try and ground the union of persons, Drummond thinks, again following South, necessarily leads to Sabellianism, whose subordinationism is essentially what the Unitarians believed anyway.[51]

The confusion is furthered, according to Drummond, by the "Egyptian darkness" of the Athanasian Creed and its use of unbegottenness for the Father, begottenness for the Son, and procession for the Spirit. Drummond argued that the language of "begotten" and "procession" indicate a fundamental difference between the persons such that "each has a peculiar and distinguishing characteristic." The Athanasian and the Nicene Creeds also contradict the Apostles Creed that says that the Son was "conceived by the Holy Ghost," thus confusing the distinction between the natures of the person of Jesus Christ.[52] The creeds therefore contradict both the scripture and themselves. Drummond thus argued that, "The three persons of the Trinity, after all that is said by the bishops and archbishops, about diversities and subsistences, modes and relations, perichoresis and circumincession, can be contemplated only as 'three distinct infinite

---

[50] Cf. Jean LeClerc, *Liberii de Sancto Amore Epistolae Theologicae* (Irenopoli: Typis Philalethianis, 1679). LeClerc, who was a direct influence on Sherlock, described the persons of the Trinity as "tres distinctae cogitationes." Drummond was right to note the influence of Descartes on LeClerc's thought, and the problems of grounding the unity of the Trinity in the "thoughts" or "modes of thinking" of the three persons. For more see Maria Rosa Antognazza, *Leibniz on the Trinity and the Incarnation: Reason and Revelation in the Seventeenth Century* (New Haven, CT: Yale University Press, 2008), 101–102.

[51] Drummond, *Doctrine of the Trinity*, 8.

[52] Drummond, *Doctrine of the Trinity*, 9.

In Essence One, in Persons Three

minds.'"[53] For the Unitarian, however, the oneness of the persons is not essential or consubstantial, but in terms of "affection and design." They have a unified purpose or mission, but this does not imply a unity of three persons in one Godhead. The doctrine of the Trinity is a chimera "full of conflicting imaginations." Once it is seen that the three are united by "moral virtue" only, their substantial "unity is abolished."[54]

The influence of aspects of the Scottish Enlightenment, particularly the emphasis on the reasonableness of religious belief, is apparent in Drummond's work from its outset. This helps explain why he was so perplexed by what he saw to be a flat contradiction with Trinitarianism. In the preface to the first edition of the work, he decried any accusations of being a follower of Arius or the Socinians. Rather, the Unitarian is a follower only of scripture "with reason and common sense, as his guides." Whatever can be judged by the reasonable mind is true and is to be accepted, whatever can be proven to be false, "no matter in what region it is found," is to be rejected.[55] Later, speaking of the two natures of Christ, he argued,

> With what consistency then, can it possibly be maintained that those two Beings are one and the same, whose attributes and offices are so exceedingly distinct, and whose grand characteristics are so far from being reciprocal, that the very idea of ascribing to the one, those which belong to the other, puts reason to the blush, and "shocks all common sense."[56]

He couples "reason and common sense" some dozen times in the treatise when dealing with core issues pertaining to the core

---

[53] Drummond, *Doctrine of the Trinity*, 9–10.
[54] Drummond, *Doctrine of the Trinity*, 10.
[55] Drummond, *Doctrine of the Trinity*, v.
[56] Drummond, *Doctrine of the Trinity*, 40.

features both of Trinitarianism in general, and two-nature Christology in particular.[57]

Carson's Irenic Response

As noted above, the Unitarian controversy was a factor in Carson's decision to leave the Ulster Synod. Even though he had joined the fledgling Baptist cause in Ireland, he was still deeply troubled over the continued influence of Unitarianism in Ulster, and openly engaged in controversy over it. Drummond was not the only Unitarian that Carson was drawn into controversy with. In 1820 he defended the doctrine of the atonement, rooting it in the deity of Christ, against the deist-turned-atheist Richard Carlile (1790–1843).[58] However, it was after reading Drummond's *Doctrine of the Trinity* that Carson penned his *A Reply to Dr. Drummond's Essay on the Doctrine of the Trinity, In a Letter to the Author* (1831).[59] In it, Carson sought to answer Drummond's objections to Trinitarianism on points of scripture and catholic doctrine. It is useful to note his response to the subject of Trinitarian personhood that Drummond had put forth, as well as what constitutes the appropriate domains of reason and common sense that Drummond appealed to. These two issues, then, will be the focus of our evaluation of Carson's response to Drummond.[60]

Though Carson was diametrically opposed to Drummond's Unitarianism, he did share with the latter an antipathy towards

---

[57] For examples of his use of "reason and common sense" see Drummond, *Doctrine of the Trinity*, 1, 56, 94, 98, 143.

[58] Alexander Carson, *The Truth of the Gospel Demonstrated from the Character of God Manifested in the Atonement. In a Letter to Mr. Richard Carlile*, 2nd ed. (Dublin: Richard Moore Tims, 1826). Cf. Joel H. Wiener, *Radicalism and Freethought in Nineteenth-Century Britain: The Life of Richard Carlile*, Contributions in Labor History 13 (Westport, CT: Greenwood Press, 1983).

[59] Alexander Carson, *A Reply to Dr. Drummond's Essay on the Doctrine of the Trinity in a Letter to the Author* (Dublin: Carson and Knox, 1831).

[60] For a thorough treatment of Carson's overall theology see Gill, "The Evangelicalism of Alexander Carson."

creeds and confessions (Drummond's "Unitarians' Creed" notwithstanding). Carson's biographer, John Douglas of Newport, Wales, wrote of Carson's view of the Westminster Confession in glowing terms: "From the time of his earliest conversion, he believed in the depths of his inmost soul that the doctrines of the Westminster Confession of Faith were founded on, and in accordance with the teachings of the Holy Scriptures."[61] However, though Carson had been raised from a young age under the Westminster Confession, and though he was ordained in a pro-subscription presbytery, he did not appear to value the use of confessions of faith later in his ministry. As noted, Carson had a high view of the bible's inspiration and authority and, as with the other orthodox subscriptionists in the Ulster Synod, saw the bible as the final authority for faith and practice. Yet like the Unitarians that he challenged over the doctrine of the Trinity, he did not make appeals to any confession for his theological commitments. The Unitarians appealed to the bible, but also to reason and common sense, whereas for Carson, the only authority was scripture. In *Reasons for Separating* he could say:

> As to the Westminster assembly [*sic*], I am neither concerned to accuse nor condemn them.—Episcopacy, presbytery, and independency have each had some of the most pious men in the list of their defenders; the christian [*sic*] then can have no safe guide but the bible.[62]

His changing ecclesiological convictions led him to a more diminished view of the authority of confessions as he observed elsewhere in *Reasons for Separating*, the Westminster Confession's statements on church government did not line up with scripture

---

[61] John Douglas, *Biographical Sketch of the Late Dr. Alexander Carson* (London: Elliott Stock, 1884), 7.

[62] Carson, *Reasons for Separating*, 84.

and so must be discarded.⁶³ Carson believed that both the Confession and the Presbyterian book of order were insufficient to truly act as guides for locally congregated churches. John Young summarizes Carson's view:

> This vast system of church-laws had not been framed to regulate the conduct of a spiritual body, like the primitive churches—for whose government the rules of the Bible would have been sufficient—but to hold together, in a state of religious formalism, the unnatural and discordant amalgam of saint and sinner, the wheat and the tares, the church and the world. Now this was precisely the condition of the people at Tubbermore. They had the 'form of godliness,' but were destitute of its power; and the legislation of a formal church could supply no remedy.⁶⁴

As an Independent, Carson believed that the only standard for doctrine and church life was the bible: "With [Independents] it is absolutely essential, not merely in church rulers, but in private members. The Bible is their code of laws; they have no other confession or book of discipline. They can do nothing without it; it must be continually in their hands; the rulers rule only by the word of God. But a man may be a Presbyterian all his life, either pastor or private member, with a very slender acquaintance with the Bible. A knowledge of forms and of ancient usages, of ecclesiastical canons and books of discipline, is the chief qualification necessary for a Presbyterian judicatory."⁶⁵ Curiously, as a Baptist, he did not appeal to the more ecclesiologically aligned standard like the Second London Confession of Faith (1689). This is likely due to the fact that Carson's view of confessions was not unlike those of his

---

⁶³ Carson, *Reasons for Separating*, 88.
⁶⁴ John Young, "Memoir of Dr. Carson," in Alexander Carson, *Baptism in Its Mode and Subjects* (Philadelphia: American Baptist Publication Society, 1845), xxvii.
⁶⁵ Cited in Young, "Memoir," xxix.

contemporary, the Restorationist Alexander Campbell (1788–1866), who, in an attempt to restore a more primitive Christianity, argued against the imposition of human authorities like creeds and confessions. Campbell was born in Broughshane, Co. Antrim, and had heard Carson preach on a number of occasions. Campbell called Carson "the finest religious teacher to whom he had ever listened."[66] Like Campbell, Carson was a significant influence for the Stone-Campbell movement and it would appear that Carson's view of creeds, though in some sense similar to his Unitarian interlocutor, was less about the role of freedom of conscience and more about primitivism.[67]

It should also be noted that though Carson was a respected polemicist who had turned his at-times acerbic pen to matters of baptism, the Roman Catholic Church, and biblical inspiration, his tone with Drummond was more openly irenic. The two had been students together at Glasgow, and Carson made regular appeals to this bond, often speaking of Drummond's upright character and intellectual ability. This irenicism did not, however, tone down the force of his criticisms of Drummond.[68] Carson's overall purpose was not simply to refute Unitarianism, but, expressing his evangelicalism, he stated to Drummond that, "I am anxious to make yourself my convert, for though delicacy, complaisance, or

---

[66] Charles F. Brazell, Jr., *Reluctant Restorationist: Thomas Campbell's Trial and Its Role in His Legacy* (unpublished PhD dissertation, The University of Texas at Arlington, 2007), 75.

[67] In his argument for believer's baptism Carson explained that his own views were influenced by Peter King (1669–1734), Lord High Chancellor of Great Britain, and his *An enquiry into the constitution, discipline, unity & worship of the primitive church that flourished within the first three hundred years after Christ faithfully collected out of the extant writings of those ages* (London: Jonathan Robinson, 1691).

[68] As W. Bradford Littlejohn notes about irenicism in an earlier context, "It is about unity in truth, for it understands that without truth, any peace will be unstable … Thus even when irenicism is the end goal of a debate, it can rarely do without some resort (often very considerable resort) to polemics, in order to show both the opponent himself, and also the undecided spectators and readers, just how serious the errors in question are." W. Bradford Littlejohn, *Richard Hooker: A Companion to His Life and Work* Cascade Companions (Eugene, OR: Cascade Books, 2015), 78.

spurious liberality may disguise the danger of unbelief, I dare not dissemble that error on this subject is condemnation."[69] Thus Carson was ultimately concerned not merely about winning an argument but winning Drummond's soul, which he perceived to be at peril.

When it came to the question of the doctrine of God and the Trinity, Carson directly addressed Drummond's "Unitarians' Creed." In his rebuttal, he expressed full agreement with the way that Drummond described the unity of God, noting classic attributes like omnipotence, omniscience, simplicity, etc. Carson noted to Drummond that "much of your creed all Trinitarians receive as essential truth." But, noting Drummond's red herring at this point, he had "always thought it very uncandid in Unitarians to labour in the proof of the unity of God, as a point of difference with Trinitarians."[70] If there is no difference, why make it out that there is one? As for the charge of polytheism against the Trinitarians, per the work of Sherlock, Carson replied that "the doctrine of a plurality of gods we hold in the utmost abhorrence." Rather, "we hold the unity of God in as strict and absolute a sense as language can express."[71] In a sense, then, Trinitarians are also "unitarian" in their affirmation of the unity of God, which is why a term like "Arian" or "Socinian" is applicable to Drummond's view, his protestations notwithstanding.

As for the Son's divinity, Carson argued that Drummond's notion that the Son's divinity is only in terms of his moral character is insufficient. "Divine" in this sense is not really divine in the theological sense, and here he accused Drummond of dishonesty in his use of language: "Is it honest to use phraseology that will be understood in a sense altogether different from that in which it is

---

[69] Carson, *Reply*, 4.
[70] Carson, *Reply*, 10.
[71] Carson, *Reply*, 11.

In Essence One, in Persons Three

explained?"[72] The proper mode of speech for the term "divinity" is to speak of that which is God.[73] Likewise, Carson argued that Drummond was being evasive in his language when he equates "person" with "being" in his argument that Trinitarianism was really tri-theism. Carson would not allow the equation of the two terms. Carson admitted that when it comes to God, "no man can pretend fully and accurately to define personality, it is absurd to allege, even as a difficulty, that distinct personality must import distinct being."[74] The two terms have never been coterminous. Regarding humans, "every distinct person is a distinct being" but this does not follow in its application to God.[75] The three persons of the Godhead are described as being distinct and yet substantially united as each subsists in the one being of God. Carson says, "I see in the scriptures, as clearly as I see the light of heaven with my eyes, a distinction in the Godhead, designated by the terms, Father, Son, and Holy Ghost, in the midst of the loudest assertions of unity."[76] The distinction corresponds to person. Any fundamental difference between the person due to their differing roles is not about the eternal Trinity, but rather in terms of the "economy of redemption" wherein the Father's wrath is satisfied by the death of the Son.[77] There is certainly a unity of purpose between the persons, but this is grounded in their essential unity as the one God.

As much as Carson was concerned to critique Drummond's theological proposals and his use of Scripture, he was just as concerned to address Drummond philosophically. As both were inheritors of the Common Sense tradition at Glasgow, the frequent use of "reason and common sense" by Drummond was

---

[72] Carson, *Reply*, 15.
[73] Carson, *Reply*, 15.
[74] Carson, *Reply*, 19.
[75] Carson, *Reply*, 20.
[76] Carson, *Reply*, 20.
[77] Carson, *Reply*, 21.

something that Carson could not let go. He agreed with Drummond that reason and common sense are guides, and were a doctrine to contradict them, the doctrine was to be rejected. He admitted, "I acknowledge reason and common sense as fully as I do the Scriptures."[78] Later he said, "I receive reason and common sense as the inspired messengers of God."[79] If the doctrine of the Trinity was thus proved to be "absurd" on the grounds of reason or common sense, he would reject it. However, Carson argued, "Truth enters its protest against what is untrue, but reason and common sense do not enter their protest against what is untrue, but against what is contradictory and absurd."[80] Carson did not believe that Drummond recognized this distinction. And for Carson, the doctrine of the Trinity was not against reason, but beyond it. Therefore, reasoning pertaining to the Trinity was not unaided as there was another authority who leads into truth, and that is the Holy Spirit, who should be recognized as a guide to reading scripture. Carson also made an interesting polemical move by putting reason and common sense in relation to one of God's key attributes, namely divine incomprehensibility. Reason was sovereign when it came to things that are generally comprehensible to humans, but it had no domain when it came to the incomprehensible. Noting the inherent contradiction in Drummond's appeal to reason, and speaking directly to Drummond, Carson wrote,

> You acknowledge that a doctrine is not to be rejected merely because it is incomprehensible, and on that which is incomprehensible reason cannot pronounce an opinion. To admit that a thing is incomprehensible, and to say it is false, is not only unwarrantable, but absurd. It is a contradiction in terms, and is, therefore, itself condemned by reason.[81]

---

[78] Carson, *Reply*, 7.
[79] Carson, *Reply*, 18.
[80] Carson, *Reply*, 52.
[81] Carson, *Reply*, 8–9.

Carson argued that the Roman Catholic doctrine of transubstantiation was contrary to reason, so it must be rejected as absurd. The Trinity, however, was a doctrine that was incomprehensible because of its supra-rational character, that is, it is not subject to the canons of reason or common sense. Thus, its status can and must be maintained because it is grounded not primarily on reason, but on revelation. Reason "has not been commissioned to promulgate any thing on this subject."[82] Carson argued that "to say that a thing is incomprehensible, is to say that reason does not understand it; but to say it is false, is to say that reason does understand it."[83] If the conclusions of reason are self-evident truths, or necessary deductions from self-evident truths, "reason ... cannot say whether the doctrine of the Trinity is true or false, because it cannot fathom the subject."[84]

If reason and common sense were applied to other doctrines, they would wreak havoc on them as well, such as the resurrection of Christ. Likewise, nature holds "incomprehensible truths" that reason and common sense, if used as Drummond does, would be destroyed. Here, Drummond is more a follower of the Scottish skeptic David Hume (1711-1776), and not a follower of Hume's greatest critic, the Common Sense Realist Thomas Reid (1710-1796), who taught at Glasgow. It was Hume who denied the possibility of matter or mind by using reason and common sense.[85] Should Drummond draw those same conclusions? Carson listed a number of aspects of nature that have what he calls "apparent incongruity" such as the relation of soul to body, the law of identity,

---

[82] Carson, *Reply*, 8.
[83] Carson, *Reply*, 9.
[84] Carson, *Reply*, 9.
[85] For Hume's immaterialism and its influence on the Irish philosopher George Berkeley (1685-1753) see Colin M. Turbayne, "Hume's Influence on Berkeley," *Revue Internationale de Philosophie* 39.154 (1985): 259-269. For Reid's response to Hume and Berkeley on the question of matter see Thomas Reid, *Essays on the Intellectual Powers of Man* (Edinburgh: Edinburgh University Press, 2002), 172.

as well as time and space. Theologically, not only is the resurrection apparently incongruous, but so is the relationship between God's knowledge with human knowledge, God's aseity, and divine eternity in relation to time and space.[86] If Drummond was consistent with his use of reason and common sense, all of these fundamental aspects of nature and God would have to be denied, just as the Trinity is denied. This is not the case with nature and God, therefore it should not be for the Trinity either. Carson argued, "So far from being the province of reason and common sense to determine that there cannot be a plurality as to personality, in unity of being or essence, I maintain that the highest degrees of reason and good sense are not entitled to give an opinion on the question, without revealed authority."

Conclusion

Much more could be said, but this short excursion into the debate between Alexander Carson and William Hamilton Drummond on the Trinity demonstrates the issues at play in Irish evangelicalism in the long eighteenth century when it pertains to the doctrine of God. Drummond rejected the authority of creeds and confessions and so employed the language of the Enlightenment and the omnicompetence of reason and common sense as a reason to reject the Trinity. Carson, also sidelining creeds and confessions, used the same language, but within an orthodox Christian framework. He too had to make use of scripture and reason, though his language is often indebted to older theological terminology that had been derived from the creeds (like subsistence, person, etc.). For Drummond, the creeds and confessions were a culprit in the development of the Trinity and so both had to be abandoned. For Carson, the creeds and confessions were so subordinate to scripture as to be effectively rendered useless. Yet while not appealing

---

[86] Carson, *Reply*, 32-33.

In Essence One, in Persons Three

directly to them, he nevertheless could not escape them. Yet in the main, he had to contest with Drummond on the same grounds.

Contributors

Jonathan W. Arnold, DPhil (Oxon) is associate professor of theological studies at Cedarville University, Cedarville, OH.

Ian Hugh Clary, PhD (University of the Free State) is associate professor of historical theology at Colorado Christian University, Lakewood, CO, and the review editor for *Evangelical Quarterly*.

Michael A. G. Haykin, ThD (University of Toronto), FRHistS, is the chair and professor of church history at the Southern Baptist Theological Seminary, Louisville, KY, and the director of the Andrew Fuller Center for Baptist Studies that operates under the auspices of Southern Seminary.

Roy M. Paul, ThD (Golden State), FRHistS, is the executive research assistant at the Canadian office of The Andrew Fuller Center for Baptist Studies.

Jesse F. Owens, PhD (The Southern Baptist Theological Seminary) serves as pastor of Immanuel Church, Gallatin, TN, and assistant professor of historical and systematic theology at Welch College, Gallatin, TN.

Jonathan E. Swan, PhD (The Southern Baptist Theological Seminary) is book review editor for *Eikon: A Journal for Biblical Anthropology* and Greek teacher at Highlands Latin School, Louisville, KY.

Steve Weaver, PhD (The Southern Baptist Theological Seminary) is an independent historian.

Scripture Index

Old Testament

Job
19:25..................................96
Psalms
2:773
51:17...............................128

Proverbs
1:20...................................91
8:22............................91, 92
8:22–24...........................92

New Testament

Mark
12:28–31.........................111
John
1:1 78, 79, 94, 95
1:4 96
1:7 96
1:14...................................78
1:1–2.................................94
3:13...................................23
4:24...................................23
8:24.................................106
20:28...............................129
Acts
20:28.................................23
20:32........................78, 79
Ephesians
1:13.................................100

Philippians
2:5–11..............................129
4:4.................................. 100
Colossians
1:12.................................. 18
1:15........................80, 87, 89
1 Timothy
2:12.................................105
3:1..................................129
3:16.................................129
Hebrews
1:3.........................80, 87, 88
2:3.................................... 38
4:12................................... 79
1 John
5:7.................................... 32

Index

A

Act of Toleration, 99, 117
Alsted, Johann Heinrich, 82
Anabaptists, 28, 46
Anti-trinitarianism, 29, 33, 34, 40, 43, 46, 60, 62, 67, 71, 76, 77
Anti-trinitarians, 99
Apostles Creed, 11, 12, 13, 32, 66, 131
Aquinas, Thomas, 79, 80, 81, 84, 85, 87, 94
Arianism, 2, 5, 9, 40, 50, 57, 58, 61, 62, 71, 87, 117, 118, 119, 120, 122, 125, 126, 137
Arius, 61, 92, 132
Arminianism, 62, 71, 121
Aseity of God, 69, 70, 71, 74, 76, 141
Athanasian Creed, 12, 13, 131
Athanasius, 12, 48, 80, 129, 130
Athenagoras, 83
Augustine, 80
Avery, Benjamin, 67

B

Ball, John, 52
Baptism, 31, 35, 36, 41, 126, 136
Barrington, John Shute, 45, 52
Bavinck, Herman, 80
Baxter, Richard, 46, 62, 64, 65, 66, 67
Beddome, Benjamin, 111, 112

Belfast Literary Society, 123
Belgic Confession, 115
Berkeley, George, 140
Best, Paul, 27, 28, 29, 30, 34, 43
Biblical theology, 36
Biblicism, 34, 64
Biddle, John, 8, 27, 28, 29, 30, 43, 64, 117
Blasphemy Act of 1697, 43
Bourn, Samuel, 118
Brinley, Benjamin, 49
Burridg, Mark, 49

C

Caffyn, Matthew, 7, 8, 24, 39, 40, 47
Calamy, Edmund, 46, 52, 53, 59, 60, 62, 67
Callender, Elisha, 59
Calvin, John, 2, 70, 75, 81, 91, 124
Campbell, Alexander, 136
Cappadocians, 80
Carlile, Richard, 133
Carson, Alexander, 5, 115, 116, 122, 124, 125, 126, 127, 133, 134, 135, 136, 137, 138, 139, 140, 141
Cattell, Thomas, 101
Chalcedonian Creed, 8
Chauncy, Isaac, 34, 36
Cheynell, Francis, 65
Christian liberty, 60, 61

Christology, 7, 15, 20, 24, 78, 133
Church of England, 14, 29, 50, 54, 57, 67, 78, 130
Church of Ireland, 127
Clarke, Samuel, 47, 48, 78, 117
Cock, Edmond, 49
Collier, Thomas, 7, 8, 9, 10, 11, 13, 16, 18, 19, 20, 21, 24
Collins, Anthony, 8
Collins, Hercules, 7, 8, 10, 17, 18, 24
Collins, William, 10
Committee of Thirteen, 49, 50, 51
Confessional subscription, 115, 116, 118, 119, 121, 123
Confessionalism, 115, 116
Congregationalists, 99
Cooke, Henry, 122
Council of Chalcedon, 39
Coxe, Nehemiah, 10
Crosley, David, 102
Cyril of Alexandria, 65

D

Deism, 2, 8, 33, 106, 133
Descartes, Renée, 131
Douglas, John, 134
Drummond, William Hamilton, 116, 122, 123, 124, 125, 127, 128, 129, 130, 131, 132, 133, 134, 136, 137, 138, 139, 140, 141, 142
Dutton, Anne, 5, 99, 100, 101, 102, 103, 104, 105, 106, 107, 109, 110, 111, 112, 114
Dutton, Benjamin, 103

E

Edwards, Jonathan, 2, 124
Emery, Gilles, 79, 80, 81, 84
Eschatology, 31
Estwick, Nicolas, 29
Eternal generation, 69, 70, 71, 72, 73, 75, 77, 80, 81, 82, 83, 84, 85, 86, 87, 88, 92, 94, 97, 108, 109, 113
Eternal procession, 108
Eternal Sonship, 113
Eternal spiration, 113
Evangelicalism, 136, 141
Evangelism, 102
Evans, Caleb, 99
Eveleigh, Josiah, 52
Extra-biblical terminology, 34
Extrabiblical words and phrases, 45, 46, 58, 59, 63, 67

F

First London Confession, 16, 21
Foxwell, Nathaniel, 63
France, Petty, 10
Fuller, Andrew, 5, 99, 143

G

General Baptists, 3, 7, 9, 10, 11, 16, 18, 19, 24, 30, 33, 35, 39, 46, 47, 50, 52, 62, 63, 64, 67, 121, 125
Gill, John, 4, 5, 60, 69, 70, 71, 72, 73, 74, 75, 76, 77, 78, 79, 80, 81, 82, 83, 84, 85, 86, 87, 88, 89, 90, 91, 92, 93, 94, 95, 96, 97, 99, 112, 113, 133
Glorious Revolution, 65
Goodwin, Thomas, 101

Grantham, Thomas, 33, 46, 47, 62, 63, 64

H

Haldane, James, 126
Haldane, Robert, 126
Hall, Samuel, 52
Hall, Thomas, 9
Hallet, Joseph, 47, 48, 49, 50, 55
Harris, Howel, 104
Hastings, Selina, 104
Heads of Agreement, 117
Heidelberg Catechism, 10, 11, 13, 14, 17, 22
Hervey, James, 112
Holy Spirit, 3, 4, 5, 9, 11, 13, 14, 15, 17, 18, 19, 20, 21, 23, 32, 33, 34, 40, 41, 42, 49, 50, 51, 63, 64, 72, 73, 74, 75, 76, 100, 101, 102, 107, 108, 109, 110, 111, 113, 121, 130, 131, 138, 139
Horsham, William, 52
Hume, David, 140
Hunt, Jeremiah, 51
Hussey, Joseph, 102
Hyde, Robert, 31
Hyper-Calvinism, 4, 102
Hypostatic union, 23, 39

I

Ignatius, 83
Independents, 29, 45, 135
Ingenerateness, 108
Irish Presbyterians, 121
Ivimey, Joseph, 103, 104

J

James I, 28
Jeffery, Thomas, 49
Jekyl, Joseph, 53
Justin Martyr, 80

K

Keach, Benjamin, 8, 27, 29, 30, 31, 32, 33, 34, 35, 36, 37, 38, 39, 40, 41, 42, 43, 44
Keach, Hannah, 40
Keech, Joseph, 32
King, Jerome, 49
King, Peter, 136
Knollys, Hanserd, 102

L

Lacantius, 80
Lardner, Nathaniel, 67
Lavington, John, 48, 50
Laying on of hands, 41
LeClerc, Jean, 131
Legate, Batholomew, 27
Leigh, Edward, 82
Limited atonement, 7
Lord Stanhope, 52
Lord's Supper, 41, 125
Lucretius, 123
Lydston, Francis, 49

M

Maguire, Thomas, 127
Manston, Joseph, 52
Marlow, Isaac, 3, 31
Modalism, 107
Monck, Thomas, 8
Moore, John, 52, 101

Munckly, Samuel, 49

N

Nevin, Thomas, 121
Niceano-Constantinopolitan Creed, 8
Nicene Creed, 12, 13, 14, 63, 70, 131
Nicene-Constantinopolitan Creed, 32
Niceno-Constantinopolitan Creed, 13
Non-subscriptionism, 121
Nye, Stephen, 30

O

Open-membership, 101
Original sin, 7
Orthodox Catechism, 10, 11, 12, 13, 14, 16, 17, 21, 22, 24
Owen, John, 2, 17, 19, 29, 34, 36, 65

P

Papists, 66, 82
Particular redemption, 9
Peirce, James, 45, 47, 48, 49, 50, 52, 55, 62, 118
Penn, William, 38, 40
Perkins, William, 81
Pluralism, 99
Pneumatology, 40
Polanus, Amandus, 86
Polytheism, 130, 137
Poole, Matthew, 29
Pope, Richard T.P., 127
Presbyterians, 3, 5, 29, 45, 46, 62, 67, 120, 123

Priestley, Joseph, 117
Protestant Reformation, 1, 2, 19, 36, 40, 70, 71, 81, 94, 115
Pym, John, 49

Q

Quakers, 40

R

Racovian Catechism, 27, 28, 34, 117
Reid, Thomas, 140
Religious liberty, 99
Revival, 2, 5
Reynolds, Thomas, 52
Ridgley, Thomas, 71, 113
Rippon, John, 4, 77
Robinson, Benjamin, 52
Romaine, William, 100, 106, 107, 108, 109, 110, 111, 112, 113, 114
Roman Catholicism, 13, 127, 128, 136, 140

S

Sabbatarianism, 31
Sabellianism, 47, 77, 79, 87, 107, 131
Salters' Hall, 5, 45, 46, 50, 51, 52, 53, 56, 57, 58, 59, 60, 62, 63, 64, 67, 115, 117, 119
Sanctification, 13, 41, 65
Savoy Declaration, 16, 21, 29, 30
Schism Act of 1714, 52
Schleiermacher, Friedrich, 2
Scottish Baptists, 126
Scottish Enlightenment, 132

Second London Confession, 7, 8, 10, 15, 16, 20, 21, 22, 24, 29, 30, 135
Servet, Miguel, 1
Servetus, Michael, 124
Seward, William, 105
Sherlock, William, 30, 34, 130
Skepp, John, 102, 103
Smith, Jeremiah, 52
Socinianism, 1, 5, 27, 29, 34, 38, 40, 57, 64, 66, 71, 77, 79, 82, 84, 87, 106, 117, 126, 127, 130, 132, 137
Socinus. *See* Sozzini, Fausto
Somerset Confession, 8
Sonship of Christ, 71, 113
South, Robert, 34, 130
Sozzini Lelio, Francesco, 1
Sozzini, Fausto, 1, 27, 28, 84
Standard Confession, 32, 33
Stennett II, Joseph, 3
Stephens, John, 49
Stogdon, Hubert, 47, 48, 49, 118
Synod of Ulster, 120, 125

T

Tatian, 80, 83
Taylor, John, 118
Tenison, Thomas, 30
Tertullian, 80
Theophilus, 83
Theophylact of Ohrid, 82
Thirty-Nine Articles, 14, 56, 59, 117
Tillotson, John, 131
Tindal, Matthew, 8, 33
Toland, John, 9
Toleration Act of 1689, 65
Tompkins, Martin, 118
Tong, William, 50, 51, 52, 57

Transubstantiation, 140
Trinitarian orthodoxy, 1, 4, 5, 117
Trinitarianism, 1, 2, 3, 5, 8, 15, 24, 34, 46, 67, 70, 77, 78, 94, 99, 129, 130, 132, 133, 138

U

Ulster Synod, 116, 122, 124, 133, 134
Union with Christ, 24, 41
Unitarianism, 1, 30, 33, 34, 66, 67, 116, 117, 119, 122, 124, 127, 128, 130, 132, 133, 136
Unitarians' Creed, 127, 134, 137

V

Vicary, Anthony, 49
Vowler, John, 49

W

Walaeus, Antonius, 81
Wallin, Benjamin, 3, 60
Wallin, Edward, 46, 59, 60, 61, 62
Walrond, Henry, 49
Walrond, John, 50, 52, 57, 62
Waterland, Daniel, 82
Wesley, John, 112
Westminster Assembly, 70
Westminster Confession of Faith, 14, 16, 21, 117, 120, 121, 124, 125, 129, 134
Westminster Shorter Catechism, 50, 56, 59
Whiston, William, 47, 48, 53, 118
White, James, 49

Whitefield, George, 102, 103, 105, 112
Wightman, Edward, 27
William III, 43
Williams, Anne. *See* Dutton, Anne

Withers, John, 49, 50, 106

Y

Young, John, 125, 135

www.ingramcontent.com/pod-product-compliance
Lightning Source LLC
Chambersburg PA
CBHW021109080526
44587CB00010B/449